RED TERROR AND GREEN

Red Terror and Green

Richard Dawson

NEW ENGLISH LIBRARY
TIMES MIRROR

First published in Great Britain by John Murray in 1920

*

FIRST NEL PAPERBACK EDITION OCTOBER 1972

*

NEL Books are published by
New English Library Limited from Barnard's Inn, Holborn, London, E.C.1.
Made and printed in Great Britain by Hunt Barnard Printing Ltd., Aylesbury, Bucks.

45001261 1

CONTENTS

CHAPTER I

IRELAND CHANGES HER MIND

WAR found Nationalist Ireland, after a century of wandering in the political wilderness, within sight of her goal. It did more; it unclasped the deadlock which the Palace Conference had failed to solve, and which threatened to produce one of two unfortunate alternatives, either such a recasting of the Home Rule Bill as would have embittered the relations between the component parts of the United Kingdom, or such an enforcement of the measure as would have caused permanent embitterment in Ireland itself. The relief of the minority at being rescued from the dire extremity of resistance was probably not greater than that of the reflecting section of the majority who realised that to set forth on self-government amidst storms of hatred would be but a poor augury of a successful voyage. But the War did even more than that. It provided Nationalist Ireland with an opportunity such as Fate seldom vouchsafes, the chance of once and for all silencing the voice of her detractors and winning the respect and confidence of her foes. And then, deaf to the wise counsels of her leader, blind to the glowing example of tens of thousands of her valiant sons, she deliberately threw the chance away. Like another Penelope, she unravelled in a night the fabric she had been weaving for a hundred years.

In the face of a decision so surprising and momentous it is not a little curious that a considerable number of men still talk and write and think in terms of the Home Rule controversy of five years ago. The columns of the Press teem with correspondence, arguing for and against partition, setting forth the respective merits of different forms of Dominion self-government, and comparing them with the American State system. Even the Government convened a Conference among the ruins of Dublin to devise a scheme that should reconcile conflicting interests in an agreed measure of Home Rule. Such well-meant activities are based on the theory – and must be abortive if the theory be incorrect – that Ireland's attitude during the last four years is the outcome of discontent with the details of the Home Rule Act, at worst manifesting itself in one of those sporadic and short-lived outbreaks of the insurrectionary movement which is endemic in Irish politics. According to this view Sinn Fein is merely the reincarnation, under another name, of the movement which called itself Young Ireland in 1848 and Fenianism in 1867.

Certain affinities of course all revolutionary parties must needs have in common: 'There is a river in Mecedon and a river at Manmouth and there is salmons in both,' But, as it is the purpose of this book to show, the affinities of Sinn Fein with the revolutionaries of the last century are entirely superficial. The resemblance indeed is hardly skin deep. It is important to note the relations between the revolutionary and constitutional agitations in Ireland since the Union. The two movements ran parallel, The extremists were no doubt ready to push their line beyond the limits set for themselves by the moderate wing of the Nationalist Party; they were anxious to move faster; possibly they chafed at and despised the caution and half-heartedness of the moderates, but they never tried to thwart or trip them up. The revolutionary vein which lay beneath the surface only out-cropped during the periods when the constitutional movement was utterly stagnant. The Young Irelanders only made their effort at times when the Repeal agitation – which they supported – had burned itself out. The rebellion of 1848 came when O'Connell's agitation had died away. The Fenian Rising came half-way between the Tenant Right and the Land League movements, when the demand for self-government had sunk to an almost inaudible whisper. The fact that, despite the existence of the Clan-na-Gael, Ireland had not, until Easter Week, had an armed rising for fifty years may be attributed to the vigour and constancy with which the constitutional section were pressing their claims.

It is even more important to note the alacrity with which the champions of independence and physical force lent their aid to the advocates of limited self-government and parliamentary methods when their own methods had failed. The man who had been 'out' on '48 '67 was the peaceful voter of 1880, giving loyal support, even in the Palace of Westminster itself, to men whom he knew were out of sympathy with his extreme views. Even the Clan-na-Gael did not disdain to provide the sinews of war for a policy which fell far short of its ambitions. The extremists acted on the principle that half a loaf is better than no bread. Some, no doubt, reflected that if they could not jump the stream they might cross it by stepping stones, but, whatever their motives may have been, the significant fact remains that the revolutionary movement of the last century never showed any jealousy of the constitutional party.

Constrast such a policy with that of Sinn Fein and mark how sharp is the differentiation. So far from showing any sympathy, even tacit, with the United Irish League, when it has not held sternly aloof, it has been actively hostile. It fought its only parliamentarly election prior to the Dublin rebellion against Mr Redmond's official nominee in 1907. Even when the Home Rule Bill was marching triumphantly through Parliament its journals were snapping and snarling at the heels of the Parliamentary Party. And then, when the Parliamentarians had triumphed, when the Home Rule Act stood on the Statute Book, and when it only needed a few months of sacrifice, not uncongenial to an ardent and pugnacious race, to procure the consummation of Ireland's dreams, this body, hitherto insignificant, whose snarling the Nationalists had treated as they might the pettish snapping of a pom-pom, brought their efforts tumbling to the ground as a mischievous child overturns a house of cards, the pride of its patient builder.

The suddenness and apparent wantonness of the catastrophe, which wrecked not only the Act for the Better Government of Ireland, but what was even more important, the visions of a new era of closer comradeship between the warring elements of the country which Mr Redmond's appeal had evoked, has generated the theory that it came through some gadfly madness seizing upon a people wearied with a long struggle for liberty, sickened by hopes deferred, and turning against leaders of whom they were tired, as the children of Israel turned against Moses beside the waters of Marah.

If this be the explanation, then the task of settling the Irish question is comparatively easy, no more difficult than fishing up a broken submarine cable, splicing the fracture and setting the electric current running through the wires again. The question arises whether this is the real explanation. It might account for the refusal to enlist, and the overthrow of the Nationalist Party at the polls – though the pertinacity and magnitude of the opposition hardly coincide with the theory of the movement being only a sudden and passing whim. But it does not square with the main facts. It does not account for the astonishing rise of Sinn Fein in the course of a few weeks from a poverty-striken body, with only one branch outside Dublin, without any commanding or notorious figures among its leaders, without a Press, to an organisation which sweeps the constituencies, establishes its own Parliament, controls the local authorities, and holds three-quarters of the country in thrall. Above all, it does not account for the Dublin rebellion and the German alliance. Rational beings do not take such measures because an Act of Parliament falls short of their desires. 'No man,' said John Mitchell from the dock, 'proudly mounts the scaffold or coolly faces a felon's death . . . for nothing. No man, be he as young or vain as you will, does this in the insolence of youth or the intoxication of vanity.'

Had these events been emanations from Sinn Fein alone, the theory that they represented but a passing phase would be infinetely more credible than it is. Great political movements, still less revolutions, are not begotten by highbrows: they are the products of flesh and blood. The antiquarian enthusiasm of Dr Douglas Hyde might create a new Nationalism inspired with scholarly ideals; the intellectualism of Mr Arthur Griffith could give it practical direction; the Abbey Theatre could invest it with a generous warmth and colour. Men reared in such an atmosphere might overthrow Home Rule, not as wanton children poking at a house of cards, but with the deliberate belief that it was a flimsy temple housing false gods, but they would have lacked the driving force that alone can generate revolutions and give persistence to great political movements.

The idea may come from above, the driving force always comes from below. It is born not of the brain, but of bodies festering in the unspeakable pollution of Dublin slums, and of blood boiling under the oratory of men like James Larkin, coarse and vulgar if you will, but all the more inflammatory for that. The force gets solidity and permanence when, behind the wrong and the demagogue, stands a directing mind, such as James Connolly's, fired with indignation and sympathy and stored with knowledge. And when from those stores of knowledge he constructs a creed in which material reforms blends with the revival of ancient national ideals and traditions and with political emancipation, then indeed we can feel that we are in face of an abiding force.

The actual situation, then, is not just a simple clash between rival Nationalists, but one very grave and complex. To hope to solve the Irish question by paper constitutions, constructed without examination of all its factors, is to try to draw the subject of a jig-saw puzzle after putting half a dozen pieces into place. Such an attempt must at best be futile, at worst it may be fatal.

It is the aim of the writer to describe the new Nationalism, not as it appears to him, but as it is conceived by its authors and made manifest by events. The new Nationalism is still in process of evolutions. Even so far as it has gone it has radically altered the orientation of the Irish problem, and therefore calls for consideration by all who hope to solve it.

To achieve the task we must follow the course of two streams of thought, starting from a common source, diverging for a time into parallel channels, and then again uniting to form the Irish movement of today. On the one side we shall find ancient Irish culture invoked to create an artistic and intellectual revival: on the other we shall find the ancient Irish politico-economic organisation being invoked as the inspiration of industrial liberty. We shall see how Gaelic decadence is ascribed to the loss of the old traditions, and how the guilt is fastened not only on English Machiavellianism, but on Irishmen, posing as patriots, but unconsciously betraying their country by setting forth their aspirations and demands in terms of Anglicised politics. We shall see the old idols of the market-place and platform overthrown, and unknown figures installed on the empty pedestal, great names besmirched and ridiculed, and names long forgotten blazoned in their place. Irish history will be presented in new perspective, in which the battle of the Boyne becomes smaller than the battle of Kinsale, in which Sarsfield has less significance than Lalor, and Thompson displaces Grattan as the moulder of Ireland's future. And finally we shall see how the New Nationalism, starting with lofty ideals of national regeneration on the old lines of the ancient culture, begins to seek its inspirations from modern sources of unspeakable corruption,

CHAPTER II

IDEALISM AWAKES

In the summer of 1893 Irish Nationalism had fallen upon evil days. The tide which during thirteen years had floated it so high had spent itself and was on the ebb. Mr Gladstone was about to retire, weary and disappointed, leaving behind him none who could bend his bow; Mr Parnell had fallen, leaving behind him a riven party, distracted by jealousies and dissensions. Yet this year, which seemed to be a gravestone in the cemetery of Ireland's hopes, has come to be described as a landmark in her progress. And all because half a dozen men met in Dublin in July and founded a society to promote the study of the Irish language.

The formation of the Gaelic League was not on the face of it a world-shaking event. Except for Dr Douglas Hyde, its founders were undistiguished men, unknown outside their own narrow circles. Its object, though respectable and interesting, did not promise to stir Ireland to its depths. Although throughout the nineteenth century archaeologists and scholars had studied the Gaelic, and although there was in existence in 1893 a Society for the Preservation of the Irish Language, the youth of Ireland did not kindle. O'Connell, the great National Leader, was a native speaker of Irish, but he refused to speak anything but English, and encouraged his countrymen to follow his example. Common sense seemed to coincide with his counsel. What a waste of time did it appear to spend time in mastering a dialect confined to a handful of people, mainly peasants, which might be used to unlock the doors leading to the learning of Europe! Goethe, Schiller, Dante, Cervantes, Racine and Molière, Victor Hugo and Dumas – who would give up the chance of reading their works in order to study the *Annals of the Four Masters* or the *Books of Ballymote and Lecain* in the original? Interesting, no doubt, they were, but if Ireland were to keep abreast of the times her people had to study languages that were living, not dead. Every argument that is used against Greek today could be used with tenfold force against the study of Irish.

The Gaelic League set itself to combat that view, and found its weapon not in philosophy, but in Nationalism. In the disuse of the Irish language it was not the loss of a dialect, but the loss of a nation's soul. Though literary in its outward manifestation and strictly non-political in its constitution, it was a system of political philosophy operating through a literary medium. Its pupose was to keep alive the Irish tongue in order that the soul of Ireland might not die. To that it postponed all other considerations. To the Gaelic League, as to other Irish parties, England was the enemy, but less perhaps because of the loss of an Irish Parliament than because of the loss of the spirit of Irish nationality. That Irish representatives should sit at Westminster was regrettable, but less because it bespoke the political subjection of the Irish people than because it promoted their Anglicisation. This doctrine, if not directly opposed to, cut clean across the theory, certainly held by O'Connell and in greater or less degree by latter-day Nationalists, that Ireland's short cut to self government lay through assimilation with British aims and ideals. To the Gaelic League such teaching was anathema. Under Home Rule, so gained, whatever it might bring of gratified pride or material advantage would be outweighed by the loss of conscious nationhood. Even were the last link broken, Ireland, unless she were an Irish Ireland, would be decadent though free.

It need not be thought that the founders of the Gaelic League had in 1893 envisaged the implications of their creed quite so definitely as this, still less that they proclaimed them quite so frankly to their disciples. Otherwise they would not have found recruits where they did, even among Unionists. The non-political character of the society was always kept in the foreground. Even in 1914 Dr Douglas Hyde, answering complaints 'from many parts of Ireland that the Gaelic League was rapidly becoming a political body,' entered a very eloquent and impassioned defence, quoting words he had used the year before:

'Suppose – which God forbid – that any one political party did succeed in getting hold of the machinery or the name of the Gaelic League and succeeded in running the League on party lines, I tell you that on that very day the transcendent significance of the language movement would fail. The entire structure . . . would fall to pieces. The language, which would then be looked upon as the appanage of a single political sect, and not the inheritance of a nation, would go down in contumely and dishonour.'

And then he continued:

'The cause of Irish nationality was too holy, too sacred a thing to be stained by the dust of warring factions or disturbed by the wranglings of ephemeral party politics. The Gaelic League was the one spot in Ireland where a truce of God prevailed, and every Irishman, no matter what colour his coat, no matter what his creed, or class, or politics, was free to enter in and enjoy the fragrance and the perfume and the flowers, and the soothing breezes which blew like balm through the enchanted gardens of Holy Ireland.'*

In this purple passage Dr Hyde no doubt enunciated the principles which mainly animated him and his fellow founders of the League in 1893, and which were then convincing to persons of politics most dissimilar. But his words were less convincing at the time he spoke them and, despite his assurance, large numbers of members left the League for the very reason against which he protested. That he was able to utter them at all is either a singular instance of self-delusion or an equally singular example of self-detachment from contemporary events. Eight years before, Mr John Sweetman, a leading Gaelic Leaguer, had said:

'Out of the Gaelic League have already grown a series of movements not only strongly political, but each and all making for a separate Irish nation, freed from every link of the British connection.'†

In a printed circular of March 4th, 1906, the Clan-na-Gael, which has always kept alive the fire of Irish Revolution, thus handsomely testified to the work of the Gaelic League:

'The work of the Gaelic League is on line with the object of the Clan-na-Gael. It is preparing the mind of the country for that supreme effort which will lead to the final triumph of

* *Irish News*, October 15th, 1914.

† *Freeman's Journal*, January 31st, 1906.

the Gael. Although a non-political organisation, and acting openly within the existing law, it is steadily creating the conditions which will make a free Ireland possible.'

Dr Hyde was at that time in America. He spoke at San Francisco, and said no word to repudiate the doctrine of Mr Sweetman or the Clan-na-Gael. On the contrary, what he said was this:

'We aim high, for we aim at nothing else than establishing a new nation on the map of Europe.'*

There was no differentiation between a spirit of nationality and political nationhood, and Dr Hyde himself seized the occasion of a public dinner, following the National Teachers' Congress as Sligo, to make the kind of nationhood he wanted by ostentatiously walking out of the room when the King's health was proposed.

Exactly how far the Gaelic League has departed from its self-imposed political neutrality it needs not further to inquire. It is as the originating, if not the immediate cause of the New Nationalism, that its foundation is justly held to mark an era in the history of Irish revolution. Even had its determination to be non-political been more deeply rooted than it probably was, there were forces at work which would have undermined it, or which would have applied to their own purposes the stimulus of the language movement.

As has been observed in the preceding chapter, a vein of revolution underlies all Irish history, out-cropping when circumstances offer a favourable opportunity, or when chance provides it with a sufficiently attractive policy. The language movement provided such an opportunity. There was already in existence another body, the Gaelic Athletic Association, akin to the Gaelic League in its inspirations, but operating in the realms of sport, and avowedly political in its nature. Its object was to check Anglicisation by reviving the old Gaelic games. Archbishop Croke gave the new movement his blessing in these words, written in 1884, the year of its foundation:

'If we continue travelling for the next score years in the same direction that we have been going in for some time past, condemning the sports that were practised by our forefathers,

* *Gaelic American*, March 31st, 1906.

effacing our national features . . . and putting on with England's stuff and broadcloths her "masher" habits and such effeminate follies as she may recommend, we had better at once abjure our nationality, clap our hands for joy at the sight of the Union Jack and place "England's bloody red" triumphantly above the green.'

The *Irishman,* an organ of the physical force party, thus endorsed the archiepiscopal sentiments:

'If any two purposes should go together, they ought to be politics and athletics . . . the exigencies of our situation force us into a perpetual war with England. . . . While fighting the enemy in the by-ways which are called constitutional, we must also maintain a certain degree of readiness to meet our enemy in the field when the occasion offers.'*

In pursuance of this patriotic policy, the Association bans British soldiers or Irish policemen, and has placed itself out of communion with the Irish Amateur Athletic Association and similar bodies. In the *Irish Year Book* for 1906 schools which confine themselves to hurling and Irish football are lauded for their patriotism, while those who practise cricket and such foreign games are held up to reprobation as decadent and anti-national.

It is easy to see how Gaelic League and Gaelic Athletic Association, both finding their sanction in the remote national past, should be drawn together, and how the more forceful body should become the dominating influence, both being guided more or less unconsciously, by the underlying revolutionary forces. In this connection it is important to observe that the Gaelic League has drawn financial aid from such bodies as the Clan-na-Gael and the American Order of Hibernians.

Within a few years there came about a Separatist revival in Ireland, manifesting itself in varying forms but with a very definite and single purpose. That it was in the main intellectual and literary is, of course, due to the inspiration of the Gaelic League. Where it marked an advance upon its parent was that it admitted politics, and did not shrink, in some societies, from hints of physical force. Thus the Literary Societies which sprang up, mainly in Dublin, Cork and Belfast, only took politics as

* *Irishman*, December, 1884.

a side line, as may be seen in the columns of the *Shan Van Vocht*, a monthly journal which was published in Belfast in the closing years of the last century. The Young Ireland Society, on the other hand, while it posed as a movement of intellectuals, had for its avowed object:

'To hasten the day when the flag for which patriots suffered and martyrs died may float triumphantly over an Ireland free for ever from English rule and domination' (Annual Report, January, 1904).

The Dungannon Clubs and the Daughters of Erin Societies were extreme in their doctrine, short in their lives, and singularly disgraceful in their methods. Their literature was obscene, and they are chiefly remarkable as having been the instruments through which Sinn Fein conducted its campaign against recruiting in the early years of the century.

Perhaps the most interesting of the bodies which sprang from the Gaelic League was 'Cumann na nGaedheal,' which was an organisation in which were combined many, if not all, of the clubs above mentioned. Its interest to a great extent lies in this, that it brings us face to face with Mr Arthur Griffith, to whose teaching it owed its existence. It reflected the phase of his political evolution through which he was passing. It was Separatist in its aims, intellectual in its inspirations, and educational in its methods. In this it took its tone largely from the *United Irishman*, a journal established in 1899, with Mr Griffith as editor, by some Dublin Separatists.

We are here in the middle of the transition period from the Gaelic League to Sinn Fein. The process of evolution had begun, and can be traced in the columns of the *United Irishman*, but it had not reached its full development. Although Mr Arthur Griffith had set himself definitely political aims of a Separatist tendency, the propagandist methods of his paper were still very largely those of the Gaelic League. In his coadjutor, Mr William Rooney, he had a man of less ability indeed than Thomas Davis, the poet of the Young Ireland movement, but of similar character and with the additional qualification that he was an accomplished Irish scholar. This combination of hard-headed Nationalism and scholarly passion was fruitful. The *United Irishman*, as has been said by an historian of the movement, acted both as its secretary and organiser; got into touch with every literary or political club of Separatist leanings, and federated them in the Cumann na nGaedheal.

But still the movement hung fire. It had its goal, it had found its spiritual inspiration, it had stirred the imagination of the youths of Ireland, it had won the sympathy and support of underground revolution, but it still lacked motive force. It was bitterly critical of the constitutional Nationalists, but destructive criticism alone can never maintain a party, much less inspire revolutionary action. Even the cry of Separation was not enough. It had been preached before so often, and had been attempted with results so disastrous, that it had become almost academic. Something more practical was needed. Home Rule, though perhaps only an unsatisfying compromise, was at least a practical and, more important, practicable suggestion. If that compromise were to be turned down it could only be in favour of some other alternative equally practicable and more in tune with Ireland's real aspirations.

Everything pointed to the necessity of producing a constructive policy. In 1902 Mr Rooney died and the movement lost the support of his literary and romantic enthusiasm. The Cumann na nGaedheal had done all it could do, it had paved the way, but could not start the traffic along it. There were signs of approaching dissolution in the Unionist Party. It was breaking up on the question of Tariff Reform, the popularity of the War which had carried it into office in 1900 was on the wane, it seemed probable that the next election would once more find Ireland able to renew her demands with some prospects of success.

Though, as indeed is natural, it is not mentioned by Sinn Fein writers in this connection, it is possible that the passing of the Land Purchase Act was not without its influence upon the development of the Sinn Fein idea. The Act was a great one and very popular, possibly the greatest opportunity ever offered to an agricultural people. It has made over a quarter of a million tenants owners of their holdings, at instalment rates for purchase less than their former judicial rents. It may be that to the enemies of Anglicisation this opened up alarming vistas of Anglo-Hibernian friendship. James Connolly, though he admits the benefits confirmed by the Act, invariably strives to belittle the share of Great Britain in the transaction by maintaining that it was nothing but an act, and not a complete act, of restitution.

Whether the passing of the Wyndham Act had any influence on Mr Griffith's mind or not, the other factors made it evident that without a constructive and operative programme the new Nationalism would be purely platonic, and Ireland's future would be directed by the Constitutional Party with the certain loss of the true national idea.

The problem he had to solve was this – to secure for Ireland legistlative freedom, and to secure it by extra-parliamentary action. His school objected to parliamentary action on various grounds, the most obvious being that any concessions that could be obtained by parliamentary methods would be in the nature of a compromise which would fall short of Ireland's ambitions and requirements. Although the most obvious, this was far from being the most serious objection. Infinitely more grave was the consideration that, by appealing to a British Parliament, Ireland tacitly abandoned imperishable rights. Even were Parliamentarianism effective, which it had not been and was not likely to be, the mere presence of Irish members at Westminster constituted an acceptance of the Act of Union and of the authority of the British Parliament to legislate for Ireland. Not only that; it had also diverted the mind of the people to political action in a foreign land and away for the historic, literary, and economic realities of their own. Political contact dulled the clear-cut edge of Irish Nationalism and promoted that Anglicisation of Ireland which was the danger most of all to be averted.

What form, then, should that extra-parliamentary action assume? Not force. Mr Arthur Griffith was too coldly intellectual and too clear-sighted to think that force was a practicable remedy. Nor had he at that time, though Separatist in his ideals, formulated in his practical mind the conception of an Irish Republic. For the moment the Constitution of 1782 would satisfy his aims, provided that the new Parliament should be not only the Parliament of Grattan, but a Parliament far more infused with the old traditions and the pure spirit of Irish nationality.

Groping after a solution which would avoid a hopeless appeal to force, he published scattered articles in the *United Irishman* on Austro-Hungarian relations. From these, in 1904, emerged a connected series of articles under the title of 'The Resurrection of Hungary'. In these articles he described the parallelism between the position of Hungary and Ireland, showed how the former had forced her freedom from Austria, and pointed his countrymen in the same direction.

This practical policy at once gave vitality to the spirit which was lying dormant in the new Nationalism. It was what Young Ireland, Cumann na nGaedheal, the Dungannon Clubs, the Daughters of Erin, and every Separatist organisation in Ireland had been waiting for. In no long time they became fused into a single organisation, Sinn Fein, 'Ourselves Alone'. Here, they believed, they had found the road to liberty, avoiding constitutionalism on the one hand and armed revolution on the other.

And Revolution, which did not shrink from arms, waited in the background and watched.

CHAPTER III

SINN FEIN

Leabhar na h-Eireann, or *Irish Year Book,* is a product of Sinn Fein, issued by a Publication Committee, of which in 1908 Mr Arthur Griffith was Chairman. The following description of Sinn Fein, published in 1909, is authoritative:

'SINN FEIN

Literally – "Ourselves". The title and expression of a movement which denies the lawful existence of the incorporating Union in contradistinction to Unionism and Parliamentarianism.* Sinn Fein declares Ireland to be by natural and constitutional right a Sovereign State, and teaches that the election of Irishmen to serve in the British Parliament is treason to the Irish State, as no lawful power exists, has existed, or can exist in that Parliament to legislate for Ireland. It advocates the withdrawal of the Irish representatives from Westminster, and the formation in Ireland of a voluntary legislature endowed with the moral authority of the Irish nation.'

The Constitution is then quoted as follows:–

'The object of Sinn Fein is the re-establishment of the Independence of Ireland.

'The object of the Sinn Fein policy is to unite Ireland on this broad national platform: 1st. That we are a distinct nation; 2nd. That we will not make any voluntary agreement with Great Britain until Great Britain keeps her own compact which she made by the Renunciation Act of 1783, which enacted 'that the

* In the same issue Parliamentarianism is thus defined: 'The name applied to the policy adopted by that party in Ireland which agrees with Unionism in acknowledging the validity of the Act of Union and accepting the supremacy of the British Parliament over Irish affairs, but which advocates the erection of a central elective local governing body in Ireland. To secure this it believes in action in the British Parliament.' It will be observed that the title 'Nationalist' is not applied to that party.

right claimed by the people of Ireland to be bound only by laws enacted by His Majesty and the Parliament of that Kingdom is hereby declared to be established, and ascertained for ever, and shall, at no time hereafter, be questioned or questionable.' 3rd. That we are determined to make use of any powers we have, or may have at any time in the future, to work for our own advancement, and for the creation of a prosperous, virile and independant nation.

'That the people of Ireland are a free people and that no law made without their authority or consent is, or ever can be, binding on their conscience.

*

'That national self-development through the recognition of the duties and right of citizenship on the part of the individual and by the aid and support of all movements originating from within Ireland, instinct with national tradition and not looking outside Ireland for the accomplishment of its aims, is vital to Ireland.'

Before passing on, one observation has to be made on the wording of Clauses 1 and 2 of this Constitution. They are as they stand out of harmony with one another, the first claiming independence, section 2 of the second speaking of a 'voluntary agreement' with Great Britain subject to her adhesion to the Renunciation Act of 1783, which elsewhere Mr Griffith speaks of as a 'Treaty'. The reason is that the wording of these clauses represents a compromise between the founders of Sinn Fein. One section favoured independence pure and simple and complete; another, including Mr Griffith, desired to base the movement on the Grattan Constitution as it existed after the passing of the Renunciation Act. This is, however, now of merely academic interest. Sinn Fein has long passed out of the phase of compromise. 'The policy of Sinn Fein today,' says Mr O'Hegarty* in this present year, 'is the old Sinn Fein policy with two alternatives. In the first place, it is based frankly on separation, with no mention of the Constitution of 1782;

* Mr O'Hegarty claims to write with authority, as having been a member of the 'National Council' formed by Mr Griffith, of the Executives of the Cumann na nGeadheal, Dungannon Clubs, and Sinn Fein itself until 1911.

and in the second place its immediate objective is the Peace Conference.'

It is probable that Mr Griffith did not contemplate a development so rapid and extreme when, in a speech of great length and, despite many inaccuracies, of great ability, he unfolded his plan at the first annual Convention of the National Council in November, 1905. He is too coldly intellectual, too lacking in warmth of passion or sympathy, to be a revolutionary chief. He is one of those who can construct revolutions, but who cannot conduct or control them. Mainly perhaps from his natural bent, partly perhaps from tactical prudence, he presented Sinn Fein as a means for social and economic reform to be attained through political independence, which could best and most consistently be achieved by extra-parliamentary action. And most of all he insisted that all reforms, social, economic, or political, should be inspired by and based upon the spirit of nationality. Thus in industrial matters he denounced Free Trade. 'It does not matter that all Europe has rejected it. England still holds on, and because England holds on, Ireland under the English system of education perforce concludes the "as-good-and-as-cheap" shibboleth must be a gospel. With the remainder of England's impositions and humbugs we must bundle it out of the country.' To Mr Griffith Free Trade is not only economically unsound, but it is nationally disastrous because it destroys the idea of separate nationality. There is no internationalism about Mr Arthur Griffith. As the apostle of national economics he holds up Frederick List, 'the man who thwarted England's dream of the commercial conquest of the world, and who made the mighty confederation before which England has fallen commercially, and is falling politically – Germany'. He deplores the predominance of agriculture and the neglect of manufacturing industry in Ireland not only on economic grounds, but because, by making her dependent on foreign supplies, it impairs her spirit of independent nationalism. He rests his indictment of the education system mainly on its anti-national character. 'Education in Ireland,' he declares, 'encumbers the intellect, chills the fancy, debases the soul, and enervates the body – it cuts off the Irishman from his tradition, and by denying him a country debases his soul, it stores his mind with lumber and nonsense, it destroys his fancy by depriving him of tradition, and enervates his body by denying him physical culture'. As proof that the funds provided for Irish education are 'invested to the children's moral and national destruction,' he says that from the primary schools come recruits for the British Army and Navy, and he describes the Irishman who Joins the Army, Navy, or Royal Irish Constabulary as 'necessarily, from that moment, the active enemy of his country'.*

There are many other counts in the indictment; no branch of Irish affairs, indeed, escapes inclusion. But enough perhaps has been given to show its tendency. Its basic doctrine is political. he clearly attaches equal, if not indeed greater, importance to he clearly attaches equal, if not indeed greater material progress, he clearly attaches eqaul, if not indeed greater, importance to the moral and spiritual results which would proceed from the awakening of the national idea. Self-centralisation, springing from and issuing in self-reliance, is the keystone of his doctrine.

It is, however, of less importance to consider the objects at which he aimed than the methods by which he proposed to attain them. Other men than he had thought the same thoughts, though not perhaps with the same definite consciousness and certainly without the same conviction that the material and political were so closely intertwined. But what distinguishes him from them is this – that while recognising the futility of physical force he still absolutely rejects that which was regarded as its only alternative – constitutional action – as treason to Ireland. Parliamentary action being therefore barred, he directed his countrymen along the paths by which Hungary, Finland, and Poland had won to the freedom they could not reach by force of arms. Ireland has to construct a national life outside the range of British administration. It would not be possible at once to withdraw the children of Ireland from the National Schools, but they might gradually be absorbed into

* In this Mr Griffith does an injustice. This is hardly consistent with facts. The *Irish Independent*, May 15th, 1905, contained a letter from Mr Seamus Macmanus, formerly a school teacher and prominent member of the Gaelic League, which contains this passage: 'The Irish youth who quits school without realising his duties as a rebel is, or should be, a discredit to his schoolmaster. . . . He felt his conscience easy in the knowledge that his salary was well and easily earned, so far, at least, as the stirring of discontent and the dissemination of rebellious opinions was concerned.'

the schools of the Irish Christian Brothers, or into voluntary schools, to be created and supported by the Irish people throughout the world. Secondary and University education would have to be reformed on similar lines, the lines laid down by Kossuth. As Hungary did, so should Ireland do in matters of law. There is no power to compel Irishmen at variance with one another to settle their disputes in British law courts. Why then should they do so? Let Ireland establish her own Courts of Arbitration, in which no barristers or solicitors should be allowed to practise 'who had devoted their time to hawking their souls for sale' in the Four Courts, or who did not renounce their practice in foreign Courts. Papineau and Deak had tried the plan in Canada and Hungary, why not adopt it in Ireland? Thus Ireland should boycott British goods and the armed forces of the Crown. She should refuse to pay taxes, not necessarily in a way to offend the law, but by self-denial, by refusing to drink whisky or other alcoholic liquor, thus depriving England of half her Irish revenue. The banking system of Ireland could be broken by Kossuth's expedient of establishing a patriotic National Bank, which lent its funds to the Hungarian people, not to the Austrian Government. But over and above all else, the Irish people should refuse to send representatives to the British House of Commons.

Too much attention cannot be devoted to a consideration of the last plank in the platform of Sinn Fein. It is the very pith and kernel of the movement, differentiating it absolutely from the Old Nationalism. The Constitutional Nationalist might be as keen on material reform as any Sinn Feiner – though it has in fact happened that the stress and turmoil of political warfare have pushed economic and social reform into the background, except when, as in 1880, an economic question gave vitality to the political movement. But the Constitutional Nationalist would be content to accept, and has accepted, material reform from Great Britain; he has, like Sinn Fein, inveighed against British misgovernment, but he has committed treason against Ireland in asking England to grant reforms. 'In the British Liberal as in the British Tory,' says Mr Griffith, 'we see our enemy, and in those who talk of ending British misgovernment we see the helots. It is not British misgovernment, but British government in Ireland good or bad, that we are opposed to.'

Sinn Fein therefore, is not an offshoot of constitutional Nationalism; it is a distinct organism. It is only because both parties claim to be Nationalists that there can be any confusion of thought on this point. When, in the sentence above quoted, Mr Griffith described British parties as 'enemies' and the Irish Party as 'helots,' he in truth grouped them into a common hostility to Ireland, for if his view be correct, the Irish helot is the deadlier enemy of the two, because by every effort at reform he locks the shackles more firmly upon his country. No social reform, no measure of self-government, however generous, gained by parliamentary action or recognition of the British connection could atone for the intolerable wrong it would inflict upon Ireland. This principle lies at the root of the Irish question as it exists today. For now there have been translated into fact doctrines which, when they were spoken, seemed to the exoteric audience fantastic utterances which marred an otherwise attractive programme if they were seriously meant, but which were probably not really serious.

It is rather curious to look back upon the comments made on the New Nationalism in its early days. The Unionists regarded it, as one writer said, 'with mixed feelings'. The political side, of course, they loathed. It appeared to them to be mad, so mad as to make it negligible, as a sort of window dressing. With the social and economic side of the programme they had a good deal of sympathy, it being a cardinal point of their creed that the real Irish problem is in the main economic and not political. They liked the doctrine of self-help, for they had ever deplored the fact that Ireland wasted in agitation time which might be better devoted to industry and commerce. They regretted that Sinn Fein, which in some respects saw so clearly what were Ireland's needs, was falling into the same error. Moreover, the Unionists were not displeased to see the way in which Sinn Fein ridiculed and belaboured the Parliamentary Party. Although the attack was delivered from a different angle and the criticism was inspired from a different source, they enjoyed the attack and agreed with the criticism.

The position of the parliamentary Nationalists was much more embarrassing and less comfortable. Writhing under the attacks, they could not venture on open reprisals. Having to keep an eye upon the *Irish World* and Mr Patrick Ford, through whom their war-chest was largely suplied, they could not denounce the robust Nationalism of Sinn Fein, while they could not accept it without a humiliating confession of error and their own disappearance from the field. Their attitude towards Sinn Fein, therefore, was rather that of a dignified wayfarer towards the small dog who yaps at his heels. Thinking it beneath his dignity to kick, he affects a lardly indifference the while he feels in fancy the creature's teeth meeting in his leg.

There were, indeed, some anxious moments when fancy seemed changing into certainty. The readiness of the parliamentary Nationalists to accept the Councils Bill, proffered them by Sir Henry Campbell-Bannerman in 1907, intensified the histility of Sinn Fein and secured from them the adhesion of many seceders from Mr Redmond's party, among them Mr Dolan, the Member for North Leitrim, and Sir Thomas Esmonde, one of the party Whips. Although the Devolution Bill was disowned by Mr Redmond and scornfully rejected by a Convention of the United Irish League, Sinn Fein had got hold of a weapon which it wielded with great vigour and dexterity. Mr Dolan resigned his seat and sought re-election against Mr Redmond's nominee. He was defeated, but only by some 800 or 900 votes. Not even the return of Sir Thomas Esmonde to the fold could disguise the fact that the official Nationalists had only a small majority, in a constituency where they had all the organisation and a unanimous Press, over Sinn Fein, which had not local papers, no organisation, and little money.

The dignified wayfarer had to abandon his contemptuous indifference and kick out; and to a great extent verified the military dictum that the offensive is the best defence. It was hinted that Sinn Fein was tainted with anti-clericalism, and the devout fell away.

Inflated by the Leitrim election Mr Griffith induced Sinn Fein to start a daily paper. It flickered for a few months and then died out. Those who worship success were disheartened by this failure and deserted. A scheme was mooted by some half-hearted Sinn Feiners to join hands with Mr William O'Brien, who was generally at loggerheads with his party – the basis of the compromise being that though there should be a Parliamentary Party it should be under the control of a National

Executive, which should decide policy and tactics, and among the latter whether the party should attend Parliament and, if so, when it should withdraw. The scheme was prematurely disclosed and pleased no one. The advocates of the policy of 'Thorough' on both sides denounced it, and none more heartily than the Sinn Fein Executive. But harm was done. On top of it all came the General Election of 1910.

As in 1885 and 1892, the result of that election gave the Irish Parliamentary Party the balance of power in the House of Commons, and as in both those years the Liberal Party promised Home Rule. Following the events above described, this was fatal to the Sinn Fein idea. The people resumed their allegiance to Mr Redmond and the rival organisation shrank to a shadow of its former self. Though the central body continued to meet, it had few branches to control. The *United Irishman* continued to appear, but it was comparatively neglected in the interest attached to the Three Years' War for Home Rule at Westminster.

The parliamentary players got all the limelight and the rest of the stage was in the shade. But while Sinn Fein thus stood idly, a super in the wings, and watched the leading man playing his part to the admiration of the gallery, its resolution to oust him, so far from being weakened by its downfall, developed in intensity. Now this is significant. It might have been expected that the set-back it had received would have tended to create in Sinn Fein a spirit of compromise; that it would have endeavoured to rehabilitate itself by joining in the Home Rule struggle as advocates of a large measure of self-government. As shown above, it had in 1905 shown some disposition to accept the Constitution of 1783. Sinn Fein might, therefore, have thrown itself into the fight in the three years' war, from 1911 – 1914, and propounded that measures of self-government as the minimum which Mr Redmond could accept, without any appearance of having renounced its own original views. Ninety-nine parties out of a hundred would have played so strong a card. Sinn Fein did nothing of the kind. It had dropped Grattan's Parliament once and for all, the lower its fortunes sank the stronger grew its vision of complete independence, and it disdained any compromise on that fundamental article of its faith, even though compromise might have smashed its enemies, the 'helots,' and adhesion to principle promised to be fatal to itself.

Let us turn back Mr Well's time machine and observe Sinn Fein as it was at the beginning of 1913. It is still, in the words of Mr O'Hegarty, 'the evolution of a national philisophy rather than a political portent. Its principles and policy are based upon ideas rather than rhetoric, and they appeal to the intellect rather than the passions'. Its doctrines are openly rebellious, but its methods are not illegal. While the political side of its programme shocks those who are well affected towards British rule, and much of its programme appears to them fantasic and fanatical, there is also much that extorts their assent, while its moral influence commands their respect.

It now remains to examine the causes which have converted such an organisation into a revolutionary movement that openly prescribes sporadic assassination and selects for its allies the vilest elements of society. To do so we must leave Sinn Fein at this point and trace the growth of another movement, long in process of gestation, but at that moment quickening into life.

CHAPTER IV

ENTER JAMES CONNOLLY

WITH the possible exception of Thomas Emmett, there is not in the whole gallery of Irish revolution a more commanding figure or arresting personality than that of James Connelly. Whatever view be taken of his doctrine, aims, and methods, he compels the respect due to a man who, while battling for a precarious livelihood on the lowest strata of society, still contrives to store his mind with knowledge; who at the age of twenty-six gives a new direction to the revolutionary movement in his own country; who was a potent force in the propagation of a creed that is now convulsing the world; who fought with ardour and ability for the class to which he belonged; and who finally gave his life in a hopeless struggle for the principles in which he believed. The history of the industrial movement with which we are now concerned is comprised in the twenty crowded years of stormy life which lie between the foundation of the Irish Socialist Republican Party by James Connelly in 1896 and his death in 1916.

That is not to say that Irish industrialism had not a history, often pitiful and occasionally violent. There were guilds and societies well back in the eighteenth century, and even in the days before the Reformation, and more than once Parliament was constrained to make inquiry into the relation between masters and men. But the movement had not great vitality Although Connelly observes that Labour was well organised in Dublin in the opening years of the nineteenth century, and was, indeed, the backbone of Emmett's rebellion, it made so little headway towards organisation that in 1895 the membership of the Irish unions making returns was no more than 17,476, divided between 93 unions. There were other unions which belonged to United Kingdom federations, or were branches of British organisations, but all told there were not more than 50,000 trade unionists in Ireland. And it is notable that in his book, *Labour in Ireland,* Connolly makes little or no allusion to the growth or decay of Irish labour organisation in the past, except the casual reference just quoted. And he himself gives as the reason that his purpose was not to write a history of labour in Ireland, but to give a record of labour in Irish history.

At first sight the distinction is not startling, yet it contains the key to the new industrialism which he founded, and explains why he launched his movement within two years of the meeting of the first Irish Trade Union Congress, which claimed to open up new vistas to the workers of Ireland. The weak point in that development of labour was to him that it lacked the idea of Irish Nationalism. True, it had asserted the independence of the Irish labour movement of British influence, and had thereby incurred the displeasure of British trade unionism, but this independence was not based on the conception of a labour movement based upon Gaelic ideas and finding its origin and sanction in Gaelic institutions.

Connelly himself explained his meaning in the course of articles, first published in the *Shan Van Vocht,** and afterwards reprinted under the title of *Erin's Hope:*

'The I.S.R.P. was founded in Dublin in 1896 by a few working men whom the writer had succeeded in interesting in his proposition that the two currents of revolutionary thought in Ireland – the Socialist and the National – were not antagonistic, but complementary, and that the Irish Socialist was in reality the best Irish patriot, but in order to convince the Irish people of that fact he must first learn to look inward upon Ireland for his justification, rest his arguments upon the facts of Irish history and be champion against the subjection of Ireland and all that it implies. That the Irish question was at the bottom an economic question, and that the economic struggle must first be able to function nationally before it could function internationally, and as Socialists were opposed to all oppression so should they ever be foremost in the daily battle against all its manifestations social and political.'

Were the practice not abhorrent to right-thinking persons, the reader might almost do well to turn down the corner of this page, in order that the above passage may be easy for reference,

* See Chapter III.

so much does it reveal that is new, so much does it explain that it is essential to understand. The very name of the book in which it appeared is significant. Erin's hope lay not only in the uplifting of her proletariat through Socialism, but through Socialism inspired by Irish ideas. While the Socialists of other lands are bidden to look wide over the great human family, overleaping the artificial lines of territorial boundaries, and studying the story of the race rather than the nation, the Irish Socialist is taught to concentrate his vision on his own country and its history, its traditions and its institutions, buried under the detritus of centuries. It is our task to trace how Connolly based his Socialism on Gaelic traditions and institutions, and propounded revolutionary methods as the result of his study of Irish history. But the real importance of the passage lies in the explanation it gives of the future relations which arose, and which exist today, between the political and bourgeois and the economic and proletarian revolutionary movements. James Connolly was, indeed, a Sinn Feiner, preaching its fundamental doctrine – though applied to different objects – before ever Mr Arthur Griffith began to move.

Thus were sown in 1896 the seeds which have sprung up into armed revolution and political complications the most involved and distracting. How they came to be sown must, therefore, be understood, and to reach a proper understanding we should have some knowledge of the factors which went to the making of the man who sowed them.

Of no man can it more certainly be said that he takes out of his learning very much what he brings to it than of James Connolly. By heredity he was a rebel, by bitter experience he was a revolutionary, by his environment he became a Socialist. His uncle was a Fenian, and in his company he attended meetings of extreme Nationalists when he was a boy in Edinburgh. Thus he faced the vicissitudes of his life in Scotland with a strong bias towards Nationalism in its insurrectionary form. And what vicissitudes they were! As a boy of eleven he worked in a bakery until his health gave way, and then he was a navvy, pedlar, and sometimes tramp, until for a couple of comparatively prosperous years he had a job in an Edinburgh factory. Then a return to his native Ireland, and back again to Edinburgh to take up the work of a dustman under the Corporation,

No wonder the iron entered into his soul and the idea of political insurrection grew into revolutionary hatred of his conditions.

Always a student, Connolly might have confined his studies to Irish literature had he been in Ireland. Being in Scotland, a country where philosophy is popular, and where at that time it happened that the study of social philosophy was attracting great attention, he, by a natural process, became a Socialist, and a Socialist of the Marxian school. There was then in Edinburgh one John Leslie, who had written a pamphlet in which the Land League was discussed from the standpoint of Socialistic Labour, and its teaching gave direction to his mind. Thus falling under Leslie's influence, he took the decisive step of his life. He had given up his post as dustman in order to stand as a Socialist candidate for the Town Council of Edinburgh; was defeated, and being out of work resolved him to cultivate Socialism in Ireland instead, and accordingly he went to Dublin, where he got work as a navvy in some big drainage operations, and afterwards found employment as a proof-reader on a Sunday paper.

Here, then, we find united the hereditary rebel, the convinced Socialist, the man embittered by experience, consumed with a sympathy for his class, less vehement in expression than his future coadjutor Larkin, but not the less deadly for being more restrained. This short sketch of Connolly's career enables us to understand what lay behind the Irish Socialist Republican Party.

But that is not enough. It remains to examine Connolly's interpretation of Irish history. It need not be examined in a critical spirit; to do so indeed would be a grave mistake. For the thing that matters is not whether Connolly's reading of it were true or false, but that it is the version which he gave to his followers. The writer, therefore, true to his self-imposed purpose, will present Connolly's views with a little comment or criticism as possible.

Bringing to the study of Irish history an hereditary bent towards insurrectionary methods, Connolly brought away from it a profound contempt for its historians and an ineradicable hostility to Nationalism of the type to which the last four generations have been accustomed. When he objects to the historians that they ignore or violate the dictum of Marx, 'that in every historical epoch the prevailing method of economic production and exchange, and the social organisation necessarily following from it, form the basis upon which alone can be explained the political and intellectual history of that epoch,' he makes a charge to which, until recently, the historians of all countries are equally open. They viewed events in a false perspective, as quite probably they were viewed by those who took part in them. But Connolly goes further, and seems to regard the ignoring of social and economic phenomena by Irish historians as wilful and of set purpose. Their misreading of Irish history appears to him to be due, not to ignorance of the true functions of the historian, but to deliberate treachery, born of the instinct of self-preservation.

The conspiracy had its starting-point in the dispersion of the Clans and the disappearance of the old system of communal land-ownership in 1649. Until the final victory of Cromwell the basis of Irish Society rested on tribal ownership of land, except within the Pale, and consequently when the tribes went to war against England they were fighting not only for political freedom, but for their land as well. With the suppression of the tribal or clan system the social and economic aspect of the conflict sank out of sight. With the passing of the tribal system and of the Chiefs of the Clans, the direction of the patriotic movement fell into the hands of the middle class – for the aristocracy were only patriotic so long as they feared that the land which was theirs by confiscation would be taken from them – and so became for the most part the idealised expression of middle-class interest. On these lines was Irish patriotic history written, and on these lines did Irish patriotism operate.

'Hence,' says Connolly,* 'the spokesmen of the middle-class, in the Press and on the platform, have consistently sought the emasculation of the Irish National Movement, the distortion of Irish history, and, above all, the denial of all relation between the social rights of the Irish tribes and the political rights of the Irish nation. It was hoped and intended by this means to create what is termed "a real National Movement," *i.e.* a movement in which each class would unite in a national struggle against the common enemy – England.'

It is not difficult to see how such a policy might inspire a constitutional programme, as according to Connolly it did, but

* *Lessons of History*, p. 5.

he goes further and sees its taint even in revolutionary movements.

'During the last hundred years every generation has witnessed an attempted rebellion against British rule. Every such conspiracy or rebellion has drawn the majority of its adherents from the lower orders in town and country, yet under the inspiration of a few middle-class doctrinaires the social question has been rigorously excluded from the field of action to be covered by the rebellion if successful; in hopes that by such exclusion it would be possible to conciliate the upper classes and enlist them in the struggle for freedom.'

As a result they failed – 'a warning to those who neglect the vital truth that successful revolutions are not the product of our brains, but of ripe material conditions.'

Connolly writes of this error of the insurrectionists as much in sorrow as in anger; when he comes to describe the career of parliamentary Nationalism his anger is tempered only by contempt. He is a political iconoclast, shattering patriotic reputations ruthlessly and pouring ridicule on the stock arguments and most telling catchwords of patriotic orators. There is no more picturesque figure in Irish history than that of Sarsfield; he has become a legendary hero of Irish Nationalism. The defence of Limerick, when, in the words of the French commandant, its walls could be 'battered down with roasted apples,' against William himself, is regarded as a national epic. Yet of Sarsfield and his men Connolly declares that 'so far from the pæans of praise lavished on them being justified, it is questionable whether a more enlightened or patriotic age than our own will not condemn them as little better than traitors for their action in seducing the Irish people from their allegiance to the cause of their country's freedom to plunge them into war on behalf of a foreign tyrant.' To Connolly the Williamite war was a disaster, not because the Catholic King was defeated, but because Ireland took part in it and so lost the chance of complete independence while 'the forces of their oppressors were rent in civil war.'

It had this further disastrous effect, that it ranged the leaders of both parties on the side of feudalism.* 'The so-called patriotic efforts of the Catholic gentry were directed to the conser-

* *Labour in Irish History*, p. 17.

vation of their own rights of property, as against the right of the English Parliament to interfere with or regulate such rights. The so-called Patriotic Parliament in Dublin was, in reality, like every other Parliament that ever sat in Dublin, merely a collection of land-thieves and their lackeys; their patriotism consisted in an effort to retain for themselves the spoils of the native peasantry; the English influence against which they protested was the influence of their fellow-thieves in England hungry for a share in the spoil; and Sarsfield and his followers did not become Irish patriots because of their fight against King William's Government any more than an Irish Whig out of office becomes a patriot because of his hatred to the Tories who are in.'

From the view-point of Connolly, therefore, the Williamite war loses all the dignity with which it has been invested by Irish patriots. Sarsfield's dying words at Landen, 'Oh, that this blood had been shed for Ireland!' became the merest 'tosh,' and dishonest tosh at that, for the shedding of it would only have served to place a foreign foot upon his country's neck in order that he might enjoy the spoil of his deluded fellow-countrymen. The only importance of the struggle which ended at Limerick in 1691 lies in this – that it stereotyped a form of patriotism, always vicious, and fatal where it was not futile.

CHAPTER V

LABOUR AND THE UNION

THREE events make the eighteenth century notable in the story of Irish Nationalism – the Penal Laws, Grattan's Parliament, and the Act of Union. While the latter event is the starting-point of the Parliamentary Movement, and Grattan's Parliament represents its ideal, the Penal Laws are invoked in well-nigh every speech to keep the flame of patriotism alight. These are the keynotes of the war-song of Nationalism. Connolly, on the other hand, dismisses them as historical incidents having no particular bearing on the Irish question as he sees it. Such importance as the Penal Laws possessed arose from the fact that they helped to place the manufacturing business of the country in the hands of Protestants; otherwise he holds them to be of purely 'posthumous interest'. They are indefensible, but to denounce them is to waste time and even some sympathy. For he points out that the effect of the Code in impoverishing the Catholics has been much over-rated.

In 1763 a Bill was introduced in the Irish House of Commons to give greater facilities to Protestants wishing to borrow money from Catholics, which would indicate that the oppressed had managed to thrive under the Penal Laws. And Connolly would almost seem to condemn the attention which has been given to these laws, as having the effect of distracting attention which would be better devoted to the working out of economic laws which caused infinitely greater misery and hardship to the people irrespective of religion, such as the famine of 1740, or the removal of the embargo on the admissions of Irish meat, cattle, butter, and cheese into England.*

'The "patriots", who occupied the public stage in Ireland during the period we have been dealing with never once raised

* The effect ot this measure was so to enhance the price of the articles as to make tillage comparatively unprofitable, with the result that small holders were evicted to establish ranches.

their voices to protest against such social injustice. Like their imitators today they regarded the misery of the Irish people as a convenient handle for political agitation; and, like their imitators today, they were ever ready to outvie the Government in their denunciation of all those who, more earnest than themselves, sought to find a radical cure for such misery.'*

In this general condemnation he includes men like Lucas, Molyneux, and Swift, although that great man had penned some of his bitterest satires on the side of the suffering people. Their agitation for the repeal of Poynings' Law appears to Connolly a mere beating of the wind, dishonest in its motive – though the dishonesty may have been unconscious – and entirely futile for its purpose, however successful. In this, of course, he runs directly counter to the accepted belief of Home Rule Nationalism. Poynings' Law placed Irish legislation under the control of the British Parliament, it reduced the Irish Legislature to a mere debating society. It is a frequent theme of Nationalist oratory, adorning many a speech and pointing a patriotic moral. To Connolly it mattered not a jot whether Poynings' Law were repealed or not; the result to Ireland would be much the same. Indeed the only difference to Ireland lay in this, that were the Law repealed the people would be plundered by Irishmen, while it remained in existence Englishmen shared in the plunder. The passage in which this theory is expounded merits quotation as typical of Connolly's position.

'In the course of time the section of land-thieves resident in England did claim a right to supervise the doings of the adventurers in Ireland, and, consequently, to control their Parliament. Hence arose Poynings' Law and the subordination of the Dublin Parliament to the London Parliament. Finding this subordinate position of their Parliament enabled the English ruling class to strip the Irish workers of the fruits of their toil, the more far-seeing of the privileged class in Ireland became alarmed, lest the stripping process should go too far, and leave nothing for them to fatten on.

'At once they became patriots, anxious that Ireland – which, in their phraseology, meant the ruling class in Ireland – should be free from the control of the Parliament of England. Their pamphlets, speeches and all public pronouncements were

* *Labour in Irish History*, p. 32.

devoted to telling the world how much nicer, equitable, and altogether more delectable it would be for the Irish people to be robbed in the interests of a native-born aristocracy than to witness the painful spectacle of that aristocracy being compelled to divide the plunder with its English rival.'* Perhaps, he admits, Swift and his friends did not confess even to themselves that this was the basis of their political creed, but he feels bound to expose the flimsy sophistry which strives to impart to a sordid, self-seeking struggle the appearance of a patriotic movement.

As with Swift and Molyneux, so with Grattan and Flood, the 'Two Harries', as they are contemptuously called by Connolly, quoting the words of a street ballad written at the time of what he calls the 'betrayal of the Irish Volunteers'. Grattan is 'the ideal capitalist statesman, his spirit was the spirit of the bourgeoisie incarnate. He cared more for the rights of property than for human rights or the interests of any religion.' 'The eminently respectable, anti-revolutionary, religious Mr Henry Grattan was at heart a free thinker, free lover, and epicurean philosopher.' He had accepted a donation of £50,000 from the Government for his 'patriotic' services, and afterwards 'in excess of gratitude for this timely aid repaid the Government by betraying and denouncing the Volunteers.'

Henry Flood fares little better. 'Flood, the great Protestant' patriot – he of whom Davis sings:

> Bless Henry Flood, who nobly stood
> By us through gloomy years—

in the Irish House of Commons of 1763 fiercely denounced the Government for not killing enough of the White Boys.† He called it 'clemency'. He is further described as a known enemy of the oppressed peasantry and a hater of Catholics, and it is charged against him that he spoke and voted in favour of a motion to pay the expenses of an army of 10,000 British soldiers to put down the Revolution in America.

Having thus stripped from these protagonists of self-government the haloes with which Nationalism has invested them,

* *Labour in Irish History*, p. 34.

† A secret organisation, very powerful in the South of Ireland, so called from wearing white shirts as a disguise. Their grievances were agrarian and their methods ferocious.

Connolly proceeds to shatter the image, constructed by popular fancy and historical distortion, of the constitutional system they brought into being. The Constitution of 1782 has been represented as an ideal to be worked for, but so splendid as almost to be beyond reasonable hope of attainment. It was the goal of O'Connell; others, claiming to be as patriotic as he, based their claim on demands less extreme. The period during which Ireland enjoyed that Constitution is depicted as a golden age, socially and economically. Irish prosperity was advancing by leaps and bounds, owing its origin to the free Parliament, and owing its end to the Act of Union.

Connolly devotes some space to the dissipation of the latter delusion. In the first place he denies that Ireland was really prosperous at all. In 1786 the Munster peasantry, then fighting against tithes, called upon the Irish Parliament to help them in their misery, plundered by the Protestant clergy in the form of tithes and by the Catholic clergy in the name of dues. Wages in Meath were 6d. a day in summer and 4d. in winter, and in 1796 the advertisement of a Charity Sermon in the Parish Chapel, Meath Street, Dublin, stated that in three streets in the parish of St Catherine's '2000 souls had been found in a starving condition'.

While Connolly, as a Socialist, is bound to hold that the economic condition of Ireland under Grattan's Parliament was bad because of the inadequate share of Labour in the wealth produced, he admits that from the capitalist standpoint, taking the volume of wealth produced as a standard, Ireland was during this period prosperous. But he stoutly denies that in any but an infinitesimal degree was this prosperity produced by Parliament. The establishment of free trading relations between Great Britain and Ireland, which antedated Grattan's Parliament by some few years, was contributory to it, but the root cause lay in an economic development outside the power of Parliament to create or destroy. The grant of parliamentary independence to Ireland coincided with great mechanical discoveries, which revolutionised manufacture, and by reducing the cost of manufactured goods gave an enormous stimulus to trade. Arkwright invented the water-frame in 1769, Hargreave and Crampton followed within the next decade with the spinning jenny and mechanical mule, the steam engine was applied to blast furnaces in 1788. Domestic industries gave place to factories, and the factories were hard set to supply the hosts of customers attracted by the new prices. The cotton and linen trades trebled their output, the iron trade was doubled. The boom held during the life of Grattan's Parliament; its end came soon after the Union, but not as a consequence of it.

The cause of the slump, as of the boom, was not political, but economic. As the inventor had created Irish trade, so did the inventor destroy it. The application of steam not only revolutionised methods of manufacture, but it diverted the process of manufacture to British factories. So long as the new machinery could be worked by hand Ireland could hold her own, but when steam came to be applied to the service of industry, the possession of coal weighted the scales fatally against her. During the debate in the Irish Parliament on the Union Bill, Mr Foster stated that the Irish production of linen was twice as great as that of Scotland – namely, 47,000,000 yards as against 23,000,000 – and he attributed this to the fact that Ireland had a native Parliament. By the year 1830, the single port of Dundee exported more linen than the whole of Ireland, and this melancholy result has been attributed to the Union. Connolly derides the argument. Scotland, he says, like Ireland, had been deprived of self-government. Why then had Scottish manufacturers advanced and Irish declined? Simply because Scotland had coal and other advantages which Ireland lacked.

Grattan's Parliament is the Mecca of Parliamentary Nationalism as the Union is its Hegira. Connolly is contemptuous of both.

'The theory that the fleeting "prosperity" of Ireland was created by the Parliament of Grattan is only useful to its propagators as a prop to their arguments that the Legislative Union between Great Britain and Ireland destroyed the trade of the latter country, and that, therefore, the repeal of that Union would lead to the re-establishment of Irish manufacturers on a paying basis. The fact that the Union placed all Irish manufacturers upon an absolutely equal basis legally with the manufacturers of England is usually ignored, or, worse still, perverted in its statement so as to leave the impression that the reverse is the case. In fact many thousands of our countrymen still believe that English laws prohibit mining in Ireland after certain minerals and the manufacture of certain articles. . . . There are not, and have not been since the Union, any such laws.'*

He proceeds to suggest the application of the Socratic method by any student anxious to pursue the study of this remarkable controversy in Irish history. Let him, he says, propound this question to any leading exponent of Parliamentarianism:

'Please explain the process by which the removal of Parliament from Dublin to London – a removal absolutely unaccompanied by any legislative interference with Irish industry – prevented the Irish capitalist class from continuing to produce goods for the Irish market.'

He will, he proceeds, get no logical answer to his question – no answer that any reputable thinker on economic questions will accept for a moment. He will get figures of exports and employment – that was O'Connell's method, which has been slavishly copied ever since. But neither O'Connell nor his successors have ever attempted to analyse and explain the process by which their industries were destroyed. One explanation only has been given – that the Union led to absenteeism, but that is 'worse than childish'. A few hundreds or thousands may have spent more, or all of their time in England, but what of the millions that remained? They, too, wore boots and shirts, and used tools. English, Scottish, French, and Belgian manufacturers throve by supplying the Irish people with goods, the Irish manufacturers alone could not. Why? The question remains unanswered.

But Connolly is not content to disprove these ordinarily accepted doctrines, he propounds a positive theory of his own which is in utter contradiction to them. It was not, he maintains, the Union which produced the weakness of Irish manufacturers, but the weakness of Irish manufacturers which made the Union possible. Had there been in Ireland a wealthy and energetic capitalist class, it would have been a barrier against corruption. Again, a strong and enterprising capitalist class would not, at Grattan's bidding, have forsaken and denounced the Volunteers when they demanded a reformed parliamentary representation and a more popular suffrage. And an Ireland controlled by popular suffrage would undoubtedly have established a stringent system of protection which, applied in time, might have neutralised the advantage which her coalfields gave

* *Labour in Irish History*, p. 45.

to Great Britain in the race for wealth.

Taking such a view of the political patriots of the eighteenth century, and the conscious or subconscious motives of the movements they directed and controlled, it is not surprising that Connolly conceived a profound distrust of constitutional patriotism and of the parliamentary institutions in which they found their field of operations. To him there was no difference between a Parliament endowed with the powers obtained by Grattan and the Volunteers and a Parliament shackled and made impotent by Poynings' Law. As to the aviator, hills and valleys are flattened into one level plain, so to Connolly Ireland's history from 1641 to 1800 presents no alternations of outline, it is a dreary level of futility, treachery, and corruption. Holding that belief, he regards all the agitation of the nineteenth century with contempt, as an effort, always fatuous and generally dishonest, to restore a system which was useless at its best, and at its worst was absolutely fatal to Ireland's cause. Henceforth he devotes but little attention to constitutional agitation, except so far as it touches the revolutionary movement, in which alone he sees hope for the regeneration of Ireland.

In his last speech against the Union, Henry Grattan, seeing defeat to be inevitable, apostrophised Ireland in a passage which has often been quoted:

'Yet I do not give up the country; I see her in a swoon, but she is not dead:

> Thou art not conquered; beauty's ensign yet
> Is crimson in thy lips and in thy cheeks,
> And Death's pale flag is not advanced there.'

So, too, might have spoken Connolly. For he sees the promise of returning life in the national revolutionary movement which came into being while Grattan's Parliament was at its zenith.

CHAPTER VI

THE REVOLUTIONARY MOVEMENT

For parliamentary Nationalism the eighteenth century contains four facts of capital importance: the Union, Grattan's Parliament, the Penal Laws, the rising of '98. The first gives it its *raison d'être,* the second its ideal, the two latter provide it with material to rouse the passions and stimulate the ardour of its supporters. For Connolly the century contains only one phenomenon of moment – the establishment of the Society of United Irishmen in 1791. In that event he sees the dawn of a new day in Ireland's life, the opening of an era of new visions nobler than the old, in that they were social rather than political. It is not the least of his charges against Parliamentarianism that, while it has made of the rising of 1798 an epic of patriotism, it has deliberately obscured and betrayed the principles of which that insurrection was the expression.

'Few movements in history have been more consistently misrepresented by open enemies and professed admirers than that of the United Irishmen. . . . The middle-class "patriotic" historians, orators, and journalists of Ireland have ever vied with one another in enthusiastic descriptions of their military exploits on land and sea, their hair-breadth escapes and heroic martyrdom, but have resolutely suppressed or distorted their writings, songs, and manifestoes.'

It may be that Connolly, bringing to the study of the United Irishmen movement a mind filled with Socialistic teaching, read into it a more reasoned and genuine expression of the doctrine of social revolt than it contained. It was probably more of a political movement than he admits, but it was certainly more of a social movement than subsequent generations have recognised. It is, indeed, only to by recognising that fact that an explanation can be found for the appearance of such an organisation at a moment when Ireland had her own Parliament, equipped with very ample powers, and when she was on the flood-tide of a prosperity to which she was unaccustomed. The influence of the social side of the movement has made itself felt in subsequent revolutionary movements, such as those in which Thomas Emmett and John Mitchell were the leading figures. And there can be no question of the influence of the United Irishmen on Connolly himself, and even, perhaps, upon Sinn Fein.

Indeed, there is so curious a parallelism between the objects of the United Irishmen on one side, and Sinn Fein and James Connolly on the other, that, were generalised inference not so notoriously dangerous, one would be tempted to say that at this point Sinn Fein and the Workers' Republic touched hands for a moment, to meet again in co-operation after more than a century. To read Connolly's analysis of the history of the United Irishmen is almost to read the story of Sinn Fein:

'The organisation was at first an open, peaceful association, seeking to utilise the ordinary means of political agitation in order to spread its propaganda among the masses, and so prepare them for the accomplishment of its greater end – viz. the realisation in Ireland of a republic. . . . Afterwards . . . the organisation assumed the veil and methods of secrecy, and in that form attained to such proportions as enabled it to enter into negotiations with the Revolutionary Directory of France.'

For the last four words write 'Germany', and the parallelism is complete, even to the detail that neither of the foreign allies selected was respectable.

Read the century-old Minutes of the first Dublin Society of United Irishmen – they might have been penned by Arthur Griffith:

'We have no National Government; we are ruled by Englishmen and the servants of Englishmen, whose object is the interest of another country; whose instrument is corruption; whose strength is the weakness of Ireland. . . .'

In the Secret Manifesto to the Friends of Freedom in Ireland it is stated that the external business of the society will be first propaganda, second communication with provincial centres and the formation of a National Convention of the people of Ireland. Sinn Fein calls it Dail Eireann.

If we turn to the social side of the programme, we find the

germs of the proletarian revolutionary movement. It teems with references to the Rights of Man and the grandeur of the mission of the French revolutionaries. 'Our freedom must be had at all hazards,' so writes Wolfe Tone. 'If the men of property will not help us they must fall; we will free ourselves by the aid of that large and respectable class of the community – the men of no property.'

From the Minutes of the first Dublin Society, already quoted, another extract may be made:

'When the aristocracy come forward, the people fall backward; when the people come forward, the aristocracy, fearful of being left behind, insinuate themselves into our ranks and rise into timid leaders or treacherous auxiliaries. They mean to make us their instruments, let us make them our instruments. . . . The people must serve the party, or the party must emerge in the mightiness of the people, and Hercules will then lean upon his club. On the 14th of July, the day which shall ever commemorate the French Revolution, let this Society pour out their first libation to European liberty, eventually the liberty of the world, and . . . let them swear to maintain the rights and prerogatives of their nature as men, and the rights and prerogative of Ireland as an independent people.'

In these and similar passages, crude as is their doctrine and turgid their phraseology, can be discerned the germ of new ideas of democracy, of internationalism and of class warfare. Of the second, indeed, the traces of a very shadowy character, and too much must not be deduced from the references to France. The Revolution was then in the minds of all, the 'Rights of Man' tripped from every tongue. The Irish, ever quick to take impression from outside, would take them most readily from a country the traditional enemy of England, and the asylum for thousands of Irish refugees. But the ideas of class interest, of what would now be called perhaps class consciousness, were assuming reality.

Before the break-up of the Confederation of Kilkenny and the disappearance of the Clans from Irish history the main lines of cleavage had been racial and religious, and so they continued for half a century. But the Penal Laws, which did maintain the religious cleavage, also produced another cleavage which cut across it. They did so in two ways. First, though it is frequently forgotten, there were Penal Laws against Presbyterians which in some respects were more efficiently applied than those against the Catholics. Next, the anti-Catholic Laws, though they were so outrageous that they remained to a considerable extent a dead letter, did have the effect of placing the industrial and commercial business of the country in the hands of the Protestants. The employers of labour were not considerate – there is abundant evidence in the reports of Parliamentary Commissions, taken early in the nineteenth century, to show that artisans were receiving not even starvation wages, but wages which had to be supplemented by the mendicancy of the family to keep them from starvation. Probably, on the whole, the Protestant workers were the worst off, for they formed the bulk of the industrial population. In the rural districts the Catholic tenantry found, as Connolly puts it, that 'the Catholic landlord represented the Mass less than the rent-roll,' and in the preceding chapter we have seen them protesting as much against the exactions of the Catholic priest as of the Protestant parson. Thus were formed other lines of cleavage – between rich and poor, employers and employed, landlord and tenant – which cut across the religious difference and forged a new bond of fellowship between the members of the conflicting creeds. Hence it came about that Wolfe Tone, who, if he were anything, was a Protestant, was for a time secretary of the Catholic Committee and became the founder of the United Irishmen, many of whose leaders were Protestants, and which numbered many of their co-religionists among the rank and file, the bulk of which represented the older faith. And it is not without significance that the Society of United Irishmen was founded in Belfast.

While, then, it is doubtful how far the abstractions represented by the French Revolution had permeated the mass of the United Irishman, there can be no doubt that in their movement can be found the first organisation on anything like a national scale of the Irish proletariat. The operations of the Oak Boys and Hearts of Steel in Monaghan, Down, and Antrim, and of the more formidable White Boys in the south, were the premonitory symptoms of the discontent which the United Irishmen utilised in furtherance of their political purpose with some suggestion that the wrongs should be righted. The accusation which Connolly makes against the parliamentary patriots is this – that while they utilised the discontent, they made no effort to remove or mitigate its causes; nay, that in some cases they resolutely refused to do so.

However far the movement of the United Irishmen may have been permeated by democratic and proletarian influence, there is no doubt that the Emmett Conspiracy owed to them such success as it had, and was in its nature much more closely allied with modern Socialism. Labour had been building up an organisation until there were in Dublin in the opening years of the nineteenth century a number of societies, friendly societies in name, but subserving the purpose of trade unions. Being illegal, these organisations were compelled to secrecy, and so became admirable engines of revolutionary propaganda and organisation. It happened also that the leaders of the United Irishmen, who were mainly of the middle class, had disappeared, and that consequently the direction of the conspiracy fell more into the hands of a lower order. Emmett himself was a social reformer of an advanced type. In the proclamation which he prepared to be issued in the name of the Provisional Government of Ireland, the first three articles provided for the wholesale confiscation and nationalisation of all Church property, and the transfer of all landed property, bonds, debentures and public securities until the National Government should be established and a national decision taken as to their disposition.

In his account of the Emmett Conspiracy Connolly mentions an incident of no historical moment, but interesting as revealing his attitude towards those whom he contemptuously calls 'patriots'. Daniel O'Connell was turned out in the Lawyers' Yeomanry Corps of Dublin on the night of the rising, and later pointed out to Mr Daunt a house in James Street which he had searched for 'Croppies'. (Croppies was a nickname for the rebels.) And Connolly then goes on to mention that he himself was shown at Derrynane, the home of the O'Connells in Kerry, a blunderbuss which he was told had been obtained by the future Liberator from the owner of a house in James Street.

A quarter of a century later O'Connell comes again upon the scene, whence he was to play the leading part, and to win undying adulation from Constitutional Nationalism and unmitigated hostility from the parties of Separation and Revolution.

Those twenty-five years, which the lawyer spent in preparation for his great political effort, were bad years for Labour. Industrial prosperity was on the wane. With the close of the Napoleonic wars came a fall in food prices, and tenants found it increasingly hard to pay their rents. Trouble developed between landlord and tenant in the country, between employer and employed in the towns. The trade unions seem to have acquired strength and organisation. They were still illegal up to 1824, but their existence was being recognised and winked at by the employers, who often found it convenient to negotiate with them. With the repeal of the anti-combinations laws, partial as it was, in 1824 labour organisation developed to such an extent that employers became seriously concerned.

The chief trouble seems to have arisen through the unions being rather close corporations, restricted in their membership, and resenting the employment of non-union men, or 'colts'.* Their dealings with the colts were largely executed through the medium of persons bearing the suggestive title of 'welters', who conducted their physical negotiations with much zeal and efficiency. Parliamentary Committees sat from time to time to examine into complaints of violence or of restraint on trade on the part of the unions. Violence no doubt there was in plenty but it was most rife in the earlier years of the movement; the less frequent calls on the services of the 'welters' were coincident with, and symptomatic of the growing influence and authority of organisation. The most elaborate and noteworthy of these inquiries was that instituted on the motion of O'Connell to investigate the 'constitution, proceedings and extent of combination by workers'.

O'Connell's action was dictated by unveiled hostility to the Labour movement. 'He stood in sober fact,' says Mr W. P. Ryan,† 'for industrial despotism and spoliation'. In the opening stages of his agitation for the Repeal of the Union he had had the backing of the working classes, partly, says Connolly, because 'they did not believe he was sincere in his professions

* In their *History of Trade Unionism* Mr and Mrs Sidney Webb describe the rules of the Dublin Trades Unions as 'abominably selfish,' a view with which Mr W. P. Ryan, in *The Irish Labour Movement*, does not agree.

† *The Irish Labour Movement*, p. 89.

of loyalty to the English Monarchy, nor in his desire to limit his aims to Repeal'.* In return for their support he incorporated the trades organisations in his Association, giving them the same rights as the regularly enrolled members. To this many of his supporters objected. The *Irish Monthly Magazine*, an enthusiastic Repeal organ, was especially vigorous in its denunciation of the industrial alliance, and wrote that it 'apprehended great mischief and little good from the trade unions as at present constituted'. It is possible that such protests from O'Connell's followers emboldened the Lord Lieutenant to proclaim a huge trade union demonstration in favour of the Repeal. An alliance of this kind, when the enthusiasm of one party was largely founded on the belief that the leader of the movement was a hypocrite, and when there was no reciprocal sympathy on the other, could not, and did not, last very long. As O'Connell gravitated more and more towards the Whig Party, then notoriously unfriendly to the demands and aspirations of Labour – he was a vigorous opponent of Lord Ashley's efforts to amend the Factory Laws – 'he gradually developed into the most bitter and unscrupulous enemy of trade unionism Ireland has yet produced, signalling the trade unions of Dublin out always for his most venomous attack'.† At last in 1837 he was Chairman of the Masters' Anti-Combination Society, and was denounced by his former working-class supporters, who hooted him in the street and broke up his meetings.

In such a spirit he moved for the inquiry of 1838, and himself took part in it. As an attack on Labour it was not a success. Acts of violence were proved, but so also was the very deplorable condition of the workers. The Committee, perhaps for this very reason, presented no Report.

To emphasise the completeness of O'Connell's hostility to Labour Connolly describes his differences with Feargus O'Connor, one of his ablest supporters and later famous as a leader of the Chartists. O'Connor held the view that Irish oppression was mainly economic and, seeing the miserable condition of the English worker, he strove to induce his leader to share his views and to unite the British and Irish democracies in a common movement. O'Connell refused the advice, although it

* *Labour in Irish History*, p. 149.

† Connolly, *Labour in Irish History*, p. 150.

promised him a large addition of strength, and the friends separated. Indeed, during the famous State trials, Richard Lalor Shiel made it one of his pleas in favour of O'Connell that he had stood between the people of Ireland and the people of England, and so 'prevented a junction which would be formidable enough to overturn any adminstration that could be formed'.

This policy of O'Connell and its motives will be variously estimated. To some it will appear admirable that he was ready to risk his position and impair his hope of securing Repeal of the Union rather than be the means of initiating a social revolution, with all its attendant horrors. To Connolly, and the men of the modern Irish Labour movement, he appears as a traitor to democracy and the champion of industrial despotism. To Sinn Fein he is a traitor to the old Gaelic language and the old Gaelic culture, and a helot in that he recognised British rule, even though he tried to abolish it.

Thus is this distinguished man, the 'Liberator', whose name was one to conjure with in Irish Nationalism, cast from his pedestal by the Irish patriots of today. To one section he is a helot, to the other a slave-driver, to all the enemy of Irish freedom. The whole Repeal movement, indeed, is held by them to have been a betrayal of the cause of Ireland. O'Connell recommended it as a link with England, he was ready to help England in 'bringing down the American Eagle in its highest pride of flight'. In saying it he was a traitor. Lord Lyndhurst, in a speech, had described the Irish as 'alien in blood, in language, and in religion'. Richard Lalor Shiel replied to him in a speech of impassioned eloquence. In one passage, often quoted, he repelled the insult by extolling the valour of Irish soldiers in England's army. Shiel held Lord Lyndhurst's words to be an insult; Sinn Fein and Connolly 'triumphantly assert the idea embodied in that phrase as the real basis of Irish Nationalism'.

CHAPTER VII

THE NINETEENTH CENTURY

To find the real thread of the revolutionary movement during this period we must turn from the town to the country. In the towns organisation was only feeling its way, and as it advanced so did violence apparently diminish. In the country, on the contrary, the organisation was singularly effective, and as it became more perfect so did the ferocity of its methods increase.

The years that followed the close of the Napoleonic wars were times of distress in Ireland as in Great Britain. As prices of foodstuffs fell, tenants could not pay the high rents fixed during the long years of war; as wheat-growing became unprofitable, farms were amalgamated into grazing estates, and in both cases evictions followed. And, strangely enough, the grant of Catholic Emancipation contributed to the trouble. That Act, which forms O'Connell's chief claim to the gratitude of Ireland, was accompanied by a narrowing of the franchise. Before the passing of the Act all tenants paying an annual rental of forty shillings had had a vote; by the Act the qualification was fixed at £10. As a result evictions increased. Landlords had previously welcomed a large tenantry, which under the system of open voting increased their political power. This inducement being removed, they were the more ready to obey the dictates of the economic difficulties above mentioned, and to reduce the number of their tenants. 'The Catholic middle, professional, and landed classes,' says Connolly, 'by Catholic Emancipation had the way opened to them for all the snug berths in the disposal of the Government; the Catholics of the poorer class as a result of the same Act were doomed to extermination to satisfy the vengeance of a foreign Government and an aristocracy whose power had been defied when it knew itself most supreme'.

The result was the famous Ribbon Movement, so called from the fact that the members of the society, when on duty, wore a ribbon round their arms. This society had been in existence some eight or nine years at the time of the Emancipation Act, and lasted, with quiescent intervals, until about 1857. Its period of greatest activity, however, was during the thirties. Its organisation was remarkably good, and the secrecy in which it enshrouded its proceeding for long remained practically impenetrable. Many parliamentry inquiries were held into the nature and proceedings of the Ribbon Society; it was denounced by the Catholic hierarchy, but it continued on its way, unmoved and unrevealed. By many, among them Sir George Cornewall Lewis, it was described as a trade union, and Connolly expressed the opinion that it was an industrial trade union for the protection of labourers and cottier farmers. That it was a combination for these purposes in certain, and it also intervened to prevent the lowering of wages and to promote the lowering of Church dues. But to class it as a trade union is an injustice to those bodies, as well as historically inaccurate.

In support of this it will be interesting to consider the obligation which candidates for initiation were compelled to undertake. For many years the terms of the Ribbonmen's oath were in doubt. Forms of obligation were produced, purporting to be the real oath, but the matter was not finally settled until the Parnell Commission. During that inquiry an oath was read to a witness, who replied that he had never heard it, though he would not swear that he had not heard something like it. While the question was being discussed, Mr Michael Davitt, an authority on such matters, rose and informed the Commission that the words were those of the Ribbon Oath. It runs as follows:

'In the presence of Almighty God, and this my brother, I do swear that I will suffer my right hand to be cut from my body and laid at the gaol door before I will waylay or betray a brother, and I will preserve and not spare from the cradle to the crutch and the crutch to the cradle; that I will not hear the moans or groans of infancy or old age, but that I will wade knee-deep in Orangeman's blood and do as King James did.'*

The words of this atrocious obligation demonstrated quite distinctly that, while the immediate objects of Ribbonism were allied to those of trade unions, it had religious and political im-

* Official Report of the Parnell Commission, Vol. III., p. 153.

plications which differentiated it from these bodies. Political genealogists, indeed, trace the lineage of Ribbonism back through the Defenders to Rory Oge O'Moore. In Ribbonism, therefore, and its satellites, the Whitefeet, the Blackfeet, the Terry Alts, the Lady Clares, we have revolutionary bodies, political as well as economic. If personal opinion may be interpolated it may be surmissed that, while contemporary writers described Ribbonism as a trade union movement in order to discredit trade unions, Connolly follows the same line in order to glorify both and point trade unions in the way they should go.

He makes it a ground of complaint against O'Connell's supporters that they denounced this Ribbon Movement. He quotes with disgust a manifesto posted in the market place of Ennis and in other parts of Clare by Mr Thomas Steele, a very ardent Repealer, in which he said, 'Unless you desist I denounce you as traitors to the cause of the liberty of Ireland. . . . I leave you to the Government and the fire and bayonets of the military'.

Connolly reprobates such language to the heroic men and women who had sacrificed all 'to win the emancipation from religious tyranny of the well-fed snobs who thus abandoned them'. And he continues:

'It is difficult to see how a promised Repeal of the Union some time in the future could have been of any use to the starving men of Clare, especially when they knew that their fathers had been starved, evicted, and tyrannised even *before* just as they were *after* the Union. At that time, however, it was deemed a highly patriotic act to ascribe all the ills that Irish flesh is heir to to the Union.'

*

Then came the Famine. It is not a story one cares to linger over, that story of suffering and blundering pedantry. But it has to be noted because of the lasting hostility to England which it engendered in the Irish race, and because of the deductions drawn from it by Connolly. He accepts the saying of the Irish Nationalists that 'Providence sent the potato blight, but England made the famine,' with this addendum, 'by a rigid application of the economic principles that lie at the base of capitalist Society'. To venture for a moment into controversy, it may be suggested that he would be nearer the truth if for the last words he had written 'that lay at the base of the Whig policy'. There have been famines since, in India and elsewhere, which have been met, even under 'capitalist Society,' with methods very different from those that were employed in 1846. It was Ireland's greatest misfortune to be stricken with hunger and disease while the country was ruled by a party which, of all those that have governed during a century and a half, was the most prolific of axioms and the most sterile of soul.

Connolly uses the declaration of Lord John Russell, then Prime Minister, that nothing must be done to interfere with private enterprise in the regular course of trade – a policy rigidly followed even to the incredible stupidity of stipulating in the Relief Work Acts that all labour should be entirely unproductive – to argue that such a policy would be impossible under Socialism, though entirely logical under Capitalism.

'Within the limits of the social system and its theories their Acts are unassailable and unimpeachable; it is only when we reject that system and the intellectual and social fetters it imposes that we really acquire the right to denounce the English administration of Ireland during the famine as a colossal crime against the human race. The non-Socialist Irish man or woman who fumes against that administration is in the illogical position of denouncing an effect of whose cause he is a supporter. That cause was the system of capitalist property. With the exception of those few men we have before named, the Young Ireland leaders of 1848 failed to rise to the grandeur of the opportunity offered them to choose between human rights and property rights as a basis of nationality, and the measure of their failure was the measure of their country's disaster.'

The Rebellion of 1848 convulsed Ireland – with laughter. Inept in conception, it was pitifully feeble and spiritless in execution. Yet its leaders were neither fools nor cowards. One of them, Gavan Duffy, became a Colonial Premier; among them were men of ability and reading; they had courage – cowards do not of their own will go the way of the scaffold; one of them, Meagher, was destined, fifteen years later, in the American Civil War, to prove himself a fighting man and a leader of fighting men. What then made of these men, mentally alert, physically brave, fired with zeal for the democratic principles of Mazzini, stirred by the uprising of the French democracy, blunderers, contemptible in council and nerveless in action? Connolly has no doubts as to the answer – respectability. Perhaps he is right. Men who would conduct a revolution for the upsetting of social order – and for Connolly no other revolution counts – must be fanatical in their creed and unscrupulous in their methods. That O'Brien and Meagher and Doheny and Duffy were neither fanatical nor unscrupulous is the unforgivable crime which arouses Connolly's wrath and sharpens his gibes. 'The chiefs of the Young Irelander,' he says, 'were as rabidly solicitous about the rights of the landlord as were the chiefs of the English Government. While the people perish the Young Irelander talked, and their talk was very beautiful, thoroughly grammatical, nicely polished, and the proper amount of passion introduced at the proper psychological moment.'

In effect he charges the leaders of the Young Irelanders with not understanding, or, if they understood, being false to the principles they professed. They were *bourgeois* mumbling democratic formulas, dreaming of rebellion but repudiating revolution, and unfit to use the material ready to their hand. Such material was there in the Ribbon Society, unrivalled for the purpose of social revolution, unscrupulous, mysterious, pitiless, 'deaf to the moans of infancy or age'. It may be that it was those very qualifications which repelled the leaders of Young Ireland, men of less callous fibre. If so, in Connolly's eyes, it was a grievous fault, bringing them down almost to the level of the constitutional 'patriots,' and grievously does he mourn it. The whole of Connolly's attitude towards the Young Irelander deserves most careful attention for the light it casts on the problem set forth in the first chapter of this book, and on the present Irish situation. Though Smith O'Brien and his friends were willing to break the British connection by force of arms, they are little better than such 'helots' as O'Connell because their aims were limited to political change, and did not embrace the overthrow of the whole social system at whatever cost of life or suffering.

And the tragedy of the failure is all the more complete because these *fainéant* leaders sinned against the light. There were men among them who saw the truth and pointed the way. John Mitchell was insistent on the necessity and policy of a social revolution which would have brought the English Chartists into the field. Fintan Lalor, a cripple debarred from physical service, was especially bitter against the policy of Smith O'Brien and his colleagues:

'They wanted an alliance with the landowners. They chose to consider them as Irishmen, and imagined they could induce them to hoist the green flag. . . . They desired not a democratic, but merely a national, revolution.'

Both these men were of the stuff from which the true revolutionist is made. But while Mitchell was fitted for the barricade, Lalor was pre-eminently the man for the council chamber, quick to grasp the broad principles and subtle in the weaving of the plans.

First of all rebels against British rule, they proclaimed that political rebellion and economic revolution should march together. How far Lalor preached this doctrine as an article of faith or as a practical instrument of rebellion is a little uncertain. In a passage in which he asserts that 'the soil of the country belongs as of right to the entire people of that country, not to any class, but the nation,' he is careful to add. 'no one has a higher respect for the rights of property than I have, but I do not class among them the robber rights by which the lands of this country are held in the grasp of Irish Nationalism.'*

And, indeed, he throws Socialism to the winds in his letter to the landowners of Ireland, in which he invites them, not to become Repealers, but to think and act as Irishmen, and conditionally on their doing so offers them 'new titles' and tells them that Ireland will remain theirs for ages. 'Allegiance to this fair island; it is your title of tenure to the lands you hold, and in right of it you hold them.' There is no trace of land nationalisation in this passage, nor in the very eloquent document of which it is a part.†

It is, however, unnecessary to speculate as to the precise shade of Lalor's economic creed, for above all things he insists on the land question as a weapon of successful rebellion.

In his paper, the *Irish Felon* – founded when John Mitchell's *United Irishman* was suppressed, and itself suppressed after

* *Irish Felon*, No. 1.

† Reprinted from the *Nation* in Sir Charles Duffy's *Four Years of Irish History*.

three issues – he denounces Repeal as impracticable and absurd:

'I mean to assert this, that the land question contains, and the legislative question does not contain, the materials from which victory is manufactured. . . . This island is ours, and have it we will.'*

Again:

'There is, I am convinced, but one way alone, and that is link Repeal to some other question, like the railways carriage to the engine, some question strong enough to carry both itself and Repeal together. And such a question there is in the land – one ready prepared, ages have been preparing it. An engine ready made; one too that will generate its own steam without cost or care – a self-acting engine if once the fire be kindled. *Repeal had always to be dragged.* This I speak of will carry itself as the cannon ball carries itself down the hill.'†

In *The Faith of a Felon* he further develops the thesis:–

'I perceived that the English conquest consisted of two parts combined into a whole, the conquest of our liberties and the conquest of our lands. I saw clearly the reconquest of our liberties would be incomplete and worthless without the reconquest of our lands – and could not, on its own means, be possibly achieved; while the reconquest of our lands would involve the other, and could possibly, if not easily, be achieved. The lands were owned by the conquering race or by the traitors of the conquered race. They were occupied by the native people or by settlers who had mingled or merged.'‡

Thus selecting the land question as the engine which should drag Repeal – and it will be noted that, while Lalor speaks of Repeal, he means complete independence – he advised that the revolution should proceed, not by offensive and open war, but by defensive measures, to be converted into open warfare should occasion offer. Tenants should refuse on principle to pay any rents at all until a National Convention should decide what rents they should pay and to whom they should pay them. Such a Convention 'ought on grounds of policy and economy to decide that those rents should be paid to themselves, the people for public purposes and for the behalf and benefit of them, the

* *Irish Felon*, No. 1.

† *Ibid.*, No. 2.

‡ *Ibid*, No. 3, July 8th, 1848.

entire general people'. Meanwhile, pending such a Convention, the people should immediately refuse to pay all rents and arrears, except any surplus of the harvest which might remain after making due and full provision for their own needs during the ensuing year. And then he formulates the plan of campaign in the event of the British Government employing armed force:

'We must only try to keep our harvest, to offer a peaceful passive resistance, to barricade the island, to break up the roads, to break down the bridges, and should need be, and favourable occasion occur, surely we may venture to try the steel.'

The Young Irelanders rejected Lalor's counsels in 1848. Had they accepted them their movement would not have been the pitiful farce it was. But, as Connolly points out, they were barred from accepting them because they were *bourgeois*, respectable, and, some of them, owners of property. Even had they followed them, they might have failed, as Lalor's plan failed when put into operation forty years later by Michael Davitt. Such speculations are profitless; the thing that matters is that it was Lalor who pointed Connolly on the road to social revolution as an instrument of Separation. The seed sown in the *Irish Felon* in 1848 only came to its full maturity after the lapse of more than half a century.

The Fenian Rising in the middle 'sixties, though as a rebellion it was far better planned and more virile than that of Smith O'Brien, was run on much the same general lines. Connolly, indeed, suggests that it had some of the implications of social revolution, and regards the selection for the post of Commander-in-Chief of General Cluseret, who afterwards commanded the army of Paris Commune, as pointing in that direction. This, however, seems to be another case of his reading his own subjective thought into a political movement. All revolutionaries meet on a plane of advanced ideas, and Cluseret was probably one of those adventurous soldiers who turn up wherever there is trouble Mr Ryan, the historian of Irish Labour, apparently disagrees with Connolly's view, for he describes Fenianism as for several years turning several of the sturdier Irish elements from immediate social issues. There was certainly no trace of Lalor's influence in the Fenian rebellion.

It is, indeed, interesting and instructive to note how completely the economic factor was excluded from the national movement in the years that followed 1848. While that abortive rising was being contemplated William Thompson, an Irish landlord, had written a book on the distribution of wealth in which he, to a very great extent, anticipated the doctrines of Marx. The teaching of Robert Owen, the Utopian Socialist, had enlisted the sympathies of many Irishmen of ability and sicial position. A Socialist Colony, on his model, was established at Ralahine, in County Clare, and is said to have achieved considerable success, until it came to an end owing to the estate having to change hands. O'Connell's Repeal agitation had failed; Smith O'Brien's rebellion had failed ignominiously – Fintan Lalor had shown the cause of those failures. And yet none of these events might have occurred for all the mark they left on the parliamentary demand for Irish self-government.

Lalor's teaching was, indeed, zealously ignored by the Parliamentarians. To admit that of itself the demand for self-government could not move the people, seemed to them a fatal confession. When Unionists quoted Lalor's words that 'Repeal had to be dragged,' they resented and denied the charge. Even Parnell, who of all the Parliamentarians is most leniently treated by the extremists, was only with great difficulty brought to agree to Davitt's proposal to establish the Land League in 1879, and repudiated – a little tardily, but still repudiated – the 'Plan of Campaign,' which embodied Lalor's proposal to pay only so much rent as tenants could afford, in 1887, and Parnell, though he fought for Home Rule in the legislative arena, was – if his assurance to the American Irish at Cincinnati were honest – at heart an advocate of complete separation.

These were his words:

'When we have given Ireland to the people of Ireland, we shall have laid the foundation upon which to build up our Irish nation. . . . And let us not forget that that is the ultimate goal at which all we Irishmen aim. None of us, whether we be in America or Ireland – or wherever we may be – will be satisfied until we have destroyed the last link which keeps Ireland bound to England.'*

This, then, was the lesson which Connolly learned from his survey of Irish history. He saw the miseries of the proletariat

* Speech at Cincinnati, February 23rd, 1880.

exploited by 'patriots' – the inverted commas are his – to further their movements, but in the movements themselves he saw no sign of a desire to alleviate those miseries – nay, in some instances he found a settled hostility to the attempts of Labour to obtain alleviation of its sufferings. Even in the revolutionary movements, though there he could discern some rays of light, he does not touch solid ground. And nowhere does he detect recognition of what is to him essential – that the social reconstruction of the Ireland of today must be framed in the mould of the old Gaelic system of communal property, or if not in the same mould – for allowance must be made for modern conditions – at least in the spirit which inspired that system.

And from the reading he turns away with the conviction that Ireland's freedom must come, not from above, but from below.

In 1896 he founded the Irish Socialist Republican Party.

CHAPTER VIII

STORMY PETRELS

THIS is not the biography of a man, but of a movement, and, therefore, only such incidents in Connolly's career during the next few years need be noticed as find a reflection in the evolution of his creed. And that there was a considerable development of his creed during the next fifteen years may be largely attributed to his sojourn in America. Before that event Connolly worked on the customary lines of agitation. He published extracts from the writings of the United Irishmen; he ran a paper, the *Workers' Republic*, which had a fitful existence for seven years, during which eighty-five numbers appeared; he organised a demonstration against the Jubilee of 1897, and some turbulent manifestations on the occasion of Queen Victoria's visit to Ireland in 1900; he twice sought election to the Town Council of Dublin for the Wood Quay Ward, and was opposed and defeated by the nominees of the United Irish League; and he lectured in England and Scotland. These energies were not without results. The movement became known; its authors, indeed, boasted most especially of their abandonment of the 'ridiculous secrecy' in which previous revolutionary movements had been shrouded, 'and in hundreds of speeches in the most public places of the metropolis, as well as in scores of thousands of pieces of literature scattered through the country, the Socialists announced their purpose to muster all the force of Labour for a revolutionary reconstruction'.*

In 1903 Connolly went to America, where he remained for seven years, during which he worked as linotype operator, machinist, insurance agent and so on, until in 1907 he formed the Irish Socialist Federation, becoming its organiser in the following year. Those four years were eventful for Ireland, for in them Connolly came in touch with the Industrial Workers

* Introduction to *Erin's Hope*, American Edition.

of the World. He then fell under the influence of Leon, another of whose disciples was Lenin.

His was an eclectic mind, quick to take impressions from its surroundings, and to apply them to the one dominant purpose of his life, political and social reconstruction. In the *Harp*, the organ of the Irish Socialist Federation, he introduced the new Labour policy for Ireland, inviting the co-operation of all unselfish men and women who worked for social righteousness. It was not at all necessary that there should be any particular trade mark. He had come to believe that the theoretical clearness of a few Socialists was not so important as the aroused class instincts and class consciousness of the mass of the workers. He was willing to work with any one, whatever their shades of view, who would advance the political and industrial organisation of Labour.

In nothing is the eclectic nature of Connolly's mind so evident as in the effect upon it of his association with the Industrial Workers of the World. He accepts the idea of the one big union, he rejects the idea of internationalism. In both cases he was evidently dominated by the paramount aim of unifying the political and economic revolution in Ireland and making it effective. The passage in which he rejects internationalism must be quoted as prophetic of what afterwards occurred:

'We propose to show all the workers of our fighting race that Socialism will make them better fighters without being less Irish; we propose to advise the Irish who are Socialists how to organise their forces as Irish and *get again in touch with the organised bodies of literary, educational, and revolutionary Irish*; we propose to make a campaign among our countrymen and to rely for our method mainly on imparting to them a correct interpretation of the facts of Irish history past and present; we propose to take the control of the Irish vote out of the hands of the slimy *seonini*, who use it to boost their political and business interests to the undoing of the Irish as well as the American toiler.'*

Up to this point Connolly's policy, extreme as it was, was capable of being applied in practice under the ordinarily accepted

* The *Harp*, No. 1. Seonini, pronounced shoneens, an Irish term of reproach, singifying worthless fellow. The first italics are ours.

governmental forms, and, unless it be very obscurely implicit in the constitution of the Irish Socialist Republican Party, there was nothing in his previous writings to indicate that his Irish Socialist Republic would materially depart from those forms. But in 1908 he produced a scheme in which the influence of the industrial extremists is clearly visible. It appeared first in the *Harp* and was afterwards reprinted in *Socialism Made Easy*, and is so important that, though lengthy, it must be stated in Connolly's own words:

'The political institutions of today are simply the coercive forms of capitalist society; they have grown up out of and are based upon territorial divisions of power in the hands of the ruling class in past ages, and were carried over into capitalist society to suit the needs of the capitalist class when that class overthrew the dominion of its predecessors. The delegation of the function of government into the hands of representatives elected from certain districts, states, or territories, represents no real natural division suited to the requirements of modern society, but is a survival from a time when territorial influences were more potent than industrial influences, and for that reason is totally unsuited to the needs of the new social order, which must be based upon industry. The Socialist thinker when he paints the structural form of the new social order does not imagine an industrial system directed or ruled by a body of men and women elected from an indiscriminate mass of residents within given districts, said residents working at a heterogeneous collection of trades and industries. To give the ruling, controlling, and directing of industry into the hands of such a body would be too utterly foolish. What the Socialist does realise is that under a Socialist form of society the administration of affairs will be in the hands of representatives of the various industries of the nation; that the workers in the shops and factories will organise themselves into unions, each union comprising all the workers at a given industry; that said union will democratically control the workshop life of its own industry, electing all foremen, etc., and regulating the routine of labour in that industry in subordination to the needs of society in general, to the needs of its allied trades, and to the department of industry to which it belongs. That representatives elected from these various departments of industry will meet and form the industrial administration or national government of the country. In short, Social Democracy, as its name implies, is the application to industry, or to the social life of the nation, of the fundamental principles of democracy. Such application will necessarily have to begin in the workshop, and proceed logically and consecutively upward through all the grades of industrial organisation until it reaches the culminating point of national executive power and direction. In other words, Socialism must proceed from the bottom upwards, whereas capitalist political society is organised from above downward; Socialism will be administered by a committee of experts elected from the industries and professions of the land; capitalist society is governed by representatives elected from districts, and is based upon territorial division. The local and national governing or other administrative bodies of Socialism will approach every question with impartial minds armed with the fullest knowledge born of experience; the governing bodies of capitalist society have to call in an expensive professional expert to instruct them on every technical question, and know that the impartiality of said expert varies with and depends upon the size of his fee.

'It will be seen that this conception of Socialism destroys at one blow all the fears of a bureaucratic State, ruling and ordering the lives of every individual from above, and thus gives assurance that the social order of the future will be an extension of the freedom of the individual, and not a suppression of it. In short, it blends the fullest democratic control with the most absolute expert supervision, something unthinkable of any society built upon the political state.'

Study of this statement of policy enables us to understand the debt which in later days Lenin confessed he owed to Connolly, and how Mr de Blacam is able to boast that Bolshevism was born in Ireland.*

The period of gestation had been long. During the twelve years which had elapsed since the founding of the Workers' Republican Party the movement had made but slow headway in Ireland, except among some of the more ardent and advanced thinkers. The accredited leaders of the trade unions frowned on the new doctrine; proposals that Labour should in its cor-

* Aodh de Blacam, *Towards the Republic.*

porate capacity take part in politics were regularly voted down at the annual Congress. The Gaelic League and Sinn Fein failed to be attracted by Connolly's appeal to the ancient social tradition of the Gael. To this Connolly's absence contributed; when he was translated to America he left no one worthy to wear his cloak. Mr W. P. Ryan mournfully speculates on what might have been had he remained in Ireland to knit together the intellectual and proletarian forces of evolution. There were, nevertheless, as he points out, influences at work which were gradually bringing the two together. Leaving out of account Connolly's extreme social opinions, there was much in his reading of Irish history – his appeal to Gaelic tradition and his detestation of the Parliamentarians – to arouse the sympathy of Sinn Fein, and men like Sheehy Skeffington and Pearse had places in both wings of the revolutionary movement.

The position at the beginning of 1907 was this. In America Connolly was studying social problems, constructing a constitution from the materials furnished by the Industrial Workers of the World, and evolving philosophic bases for his theories. But that alone was not enough. The philosopher and theorist can point the way, but he cannot set the mass moving along it. To do that requires qualities in which Connolly was then deficient, if indeed he ever fully acquired them. He had his sympathies, but he repressed them too rigidly; he was too much the thinker, too precise in facts, too logical, ever to become the effective mover of men.

At this moment such a man stepped upon the Irish stage, a man knowing little of philosopy and caring less, heedless of the past, reckless of the future, looking only at the present, and seeing it through eyes glowing with revolutionary fire – no logician, inconsequent, perhaps sometimes incoherent in argument, but gifted with burning speech, violent, coarse, but singularly effective with the people to whom he spoke. Like Connolly, James Larkin was a revolutionary by instinct and bitter experiences in the depths, depths lower than ever Connolly sounded, and a rebel against British rule by inheritance from his father, one of Davitt's comrades in the abortive Fenian plot against Chester Castle.

Whether he was attracted by it or whether he created it, wherever Larkin went there was generally trouble. He came to

Belfast early in 1907, and before the year was out there were serious strikes in that city, riots, military and police intervention, and shooting.

From Belfast as a centre Larkin opened up a campaign in Dublin. He chose for his field of operations the trades at the very bottom of the social scale – the dockers, carriers and casual workers, who were unorganised, neglected by the skilled artisans, and who existed in the most appalling surroundings. To read of these Dublin slums in a cold official Report is to burn with anger, to visit them is to blush with shame for the unhappy people who have to be seen by their fellow-men in such unspeakable degradation. It is not surprising that to these men Larkin came in the guise of a missionary, speaking to them in the language they knew and could understand, and all the more effective because he himself had passed through the fire. As the result of his mission, and aided by a strike in Cork, in which he, of course, took a hand, the Irish Transport and General Workers' Union was formed in 1908. It was destined in later years to become the dominant factor in the Irish Labour Movement.

Meanwhile in the rural districts there was a growing unrest such as has so often in Irish history indicated the coming of revolutionary storms. Although the cattle-driving movement never attained the dimensions of the Land League Campaign, and was free from the savagery of the White Boy and Ribbon operations, it caused much suffering and loss to its victims, who were very largely of the small landowning and tenant class It is here mentioned, not as a factor in the larger events which followed, but as indicating a general restlessness which furthered the purposes of those who were aiming at a social upheaval. It is also worth noticing because its author, Mr Ginnell, who then sat in Parliament as a Nationalist, took the occasion to denounce the Parliamentary Nationalists in unsparing language. The United Irish League was, he declared, corrupt and tyrannical. Its method of selecting candidates was a 'brazen imposture'. The people were enslaved by corrupt leaders, misrepresented by men who were themselves the slaves of others; leaders did not dare to be honest lest their personal character should be taken from them, the voters were the helpless tools of men with private axes to grind, and public life was abhorrent to decent men.*

It must have been about this time that Connolly, as Mr Ryan tells us, came to the conclusion that his migration to America had been the biggest mistake of his life. He must have felt that theorising and philosophising in America was waste of time while the leaven was fermenting so rapidly in the loaf at home, and that it was nearly time for him to return and take a hand in the game he had started so long before. As a preliminary he transferred his paper, the *Harp*, to Ireland, in January, 1910, when it was published from the office of the *Irish Nation*, with Larkin as sub-editor. Thus the men of theory and action had come together, the one complementary to the other, a rare combination for the work they had in hand.

In the Irish edition of the paper he followed up his American policy, laying less stress on theoretical Socialism than on the development of class consciousness. True to the principle he once enunciated, that 'the true revolutionist should ever call into action on his side the entire sum of all the forces and factors of political and social discontent,' he appealed to all who desired political change to co-operate with him in his aims. To some extent he succeeded. Among the disciples of Sinn Fein were some ardent spirits who chafed against the impotence of that body and welcomed a movement more virile and promising of success. Attracted in the first instance by these qualities, they gradually became more thoroughly impregnated with Connolly's economic doctrines, and thus became liaison officers between the intellectual and physical sides of the movement.

Within six months of taking over the direction of the *Harp*, Larkin, as might be expected, found himself faced with about half a dozen libel actions, and Connolly returned to Ireland. From that moment, though the *Harp* vanished before the coming legal storm, events began to move. Under Connolly's influence Larkin became more circumspect, under Larkin's influence Connolly proclaimed the policy of 'less philosophising and more fighting'. In pursuance of that dictum he announced and applied the doctrine of the sympathetic strike as a prelude to the establishment of the One Big Union. As an organiser of the Industrial Workers of the World, he wrote in the *New Age*, he had reached the conclusion that the interests of one were

* *Land and Liberty*, Laurence Ginnell, M.P.

the interests of all, that the hope of victory lay in sudden and unexpected action, and that 'no consideration of a contract with a section of the capitalist class absolved any section of us from the duty of taking instant action to protect other sections when said sections were in danger from the capitalist enemy'. He realised that the workers would sustain many defeats, and that their victories would often be ephemeral, but 'the resultant moral effect would be of incalculable value to the character and the mental attitude of our class towards their rulers'.

Acting on these lines, there were continual strikes throughout the country, until the Transport Union and its leaders aroused the animosity not only of employers, farmers, and clergy, but even of the Dublin Trades Council itself. Liberty Hall, the headquarters of the Union, came to be looked upon much as, in these later days, one might regard a poison gas manufactory. But the Ishmaelites pursued their course, not only undisturbed, but encouraged by the hostility they had aroused. In 1911 they produced the *Irish Worker*, to replace the defunct *Harp*, in which Larkin wrote a 'Call to Arms' which, though a somewhat colourless example of his style, may be quoted in part as indicative of his method:

'During the recent skirmish between Labour and Capitalism in Ireland you got a foretaste of how your bowelless masters regard you. Their kept Press spewed foul lies, innuendoes, and gave space to knaves of our own class for the purpose of garotting our glorious movement. At present you spend your lives in sordid labour and have your abode in filthy slums; your children hunger and your masters say your slavery must endure for ever. If you would come out of bondage, yourself must forge the weapons and fight the grim battle.'

Coincidently with these activities the allies addressed themselves to the task of making Labour a political force. As mentioned before, the Trade Union Congress had always rejected the idea, but Connolly set to work to break down the opposition. A Dublin Labour Party was formed 'to unite the forces of Labour in order to secure the election of independent Labour representatives to Parliament and local government bodies'. The idea caught on: in the first municipal election after its formation the new party secured the election of nine of its candidates, including Larkin, and at the Clonmel Labour Congress of 1912 a motion to found an Irish Labour Party, independent of all other parties, was carried by a majority of more than two to one. From that time the annual Congress meetings became more and more engaged with political questions, both national and international, and entered into relations with the British Labour Party with reference to questions before Parliament, more especially those relating to Ireland. During 1912 nominees of the Labour Party secured seats in many towns, including Belfast, Cork, Sligo, Wexford, and Waterford, and in the following year the title of the organisation was changed to Irish Trade Union Congress and Labour Party.

Into the great Dublin Strike of 1913 we do not propose to enter in detail. It was a desperate struggle, fought out through many months with fierce determination on both sides. Every conceivable weapon, even including religion, was brought into play. There were rights and wrongs on both sides, both sides committed errors, and neither could claim a decisive victory. From our present point of view, however, its importance lies in this, that 'it was the great turning point in the history of the working class in Ireland, and helped to give the workers of Ireland their place in the front ranks of the world army of militant and insurgent Labour'.*

It was, indeed, in the nature of a rehearsal for the greater tragedy to be played three years later. During the struggle the strikers had come into frequent conflict with the police and had suffered heavily. It was suggested that the workers should be armed and, acting on the suggestion, Connolly conceived the idea of the Citizen Army, which was organised by Captain White, son of the defender of Ladysmith.

* *Ireland at Berne.* Reports presented to the International Labour and Socialist Conference held at Berne, February, 1919. Issued by the authority of the Irish Labour Party and Trade Union Congress.

CHAPTER IX

UNDERCURRENTS

We have now followed from their sources to the year 1913 two revolutionary currents, the one a brawling torrent, the other a sedate and sluggish stream, destined soon to meet though not for several years to mingle; we have seen how the proletarian torrent spent itself in its mad rush, and it now remains to see how the sluggish intellectual movement stood at the opening of that year. And here we approach the realm of inference. Hitherto it has been possible to describe the policy and objects of Sinn Fein and Labour in the words of its accredited leaders. Henceforth there are undercurrents, the influence of which is apparent, but which are of necessity obscure. Both Sinn Fein and Connolly, as we have seen, prided themselves on their publicity, but there came a time when publicity became impossible for them, as it becomes impossible some time or another for those who are plotting revolution.

At what precise moment Sinn Fein began to contemplate revolution it is impossible to say. Rebellious it had always been in theory, but it is one thing to contemplate revolt as an abstract proposition and another to take the grim measures to put into operation. When 1913 opened, and with it the second stage of the fight over the Home Rule Bill, the Sinn Fein leaders certainly did not contemplate armed rebellion. To begin with, they were not in a position to do so, and they knew it. The excitement of the parliamentary fight was driving everything else out of the minds of the people. Sinn Fein was neglected, impotent and penniless. It is important to note the latter fact in view of the sudden affluence which so soon followed. Its leaders hated the Parliamentarians and detested the Home Rule Bill. Mr Redmond-Howard, indeed, tries to minimise their opposition to his uncle's policy. He says that Sinn Fein withdrew from opposition lest it should be said that in a moment of acute difficulty it had hampered any Irishman in winning any liberties for Ireland, and its daily paper was withdrawn.* Mr Hegarty takes a different view of its action. The daily paper was withdrawn, not to save Mr Redmond embarrassment, but for lack of funds; the Sinn Feiners marked time because they knew well that 'the issue would be unfavourable to the continued adhesion of the contry to the Parliamentarian policy'.† Both writers agreed that Sinn Fein was giving Mr Redmond a chance, but according to Mr O'Hegarty it was a chance to hang himself, not to win Ireland's liberties. Nor is this conclusion vitiated by an article by Mr Arthur Griffith in the *Irish Review* of May, 1912. In that article he condemned the Home Rule Bill, but added, 'if the Bill be amended to give Ireland real control of her soil and taxes and power of initiation in her legislation, I shall welcome its passage as a measure for the improvement of conditions in Ireland, and a step clearing the way to a final settlement between the two nations.'

This, after all, was no more than a reassertion of his willingness to accept Grattan's Parliament, which, as we have seen, he had induced Sinn Fein to embody in its programme. But, though Mr Griffith held that comparatively moderate view himself, it was with difficulty that he got his colleagues to accept it in 1905, and it is more than doubtful if he could have got a majority for it in 1913. For during the intervening period Sinn Fein had shed many of its most moderate elements. Some had gone owing to the cry that Sinn Fein was anti-clerical; others had retired discouraged by the slump in its fortunes after the short-lived boom of 1907–8; many left to join Mr Redmond when the Home Rule Bill was introduced, on the ground that half a loaf was better than no bread, and that, though the Bill itself might not be wholly satisfactory, it would provide a jumping-off place for further developments. And, while these influences were at work within the party to eliminate the moderates, there were external influences at work to make those who remained more extreme in their views. Some fell under the influence of Connolly's movement, attracted by his presentation of Irish history, his appeal to the old Gaelic social system, and his insistence on the principle of nationality. Others, whom his extreme communistic doctrines repelled, fell under

* *Six Days of the Irish Republic*, p. 76.

† *Sinn Fein*, p. 38.

American Fenian influence, always ready to seize every chance to foment trouble in Ireland. It is notable that during this period the extreme Irish Party in America was divided into two sections, that represented by the *Irish World*, backing Mr Redmond, the other, represented by the *Gaelic American*, supporting Sinn Fein.

While, therefore, at the beginning of 1913 Sinn Fein was inconspicious, penniless, and infinitely less strong than it had been five years earlier, and while Mr Griffith's views remained substantially unchanged, it is certain that in spirit it was more unyielding and uncompromising, and that it was moving, though perhaps very slowly, from intellectual theories to more practical measures.

It was at this juncture the Sir Roger Casement came to Ireland, on his retirement from the British Consular Service. No more sinister figure ever stepped upon the Irish stage than this British officer who came to play a dual *rôle*, that of an Irish rebel and a German agent. Whether he was more the Irish patriot of the German agent it is not easy to decide, nor is it necessary, for it was Casement's good fortune to find his domestic policy and his foreign obligations moving together towards a common goal – the liberation of Ireland and the placing of Great Britain under the heel of Germany.

In respect of Irish politics Casement's proclivites were akin to those of the Gaelic League and Sinn Fein. His entry into the national arena roughly synchronised with the foundation of the League with whose literary aims he was in sympathy. He was one of those who from this beginning developed into hostility to the Parliamentary Movement and to British rule, of which he was nowhere much enamoured. During his trial it was suggested both by himself and his counsel that the action which brought him to the scaffold was the action of a patriot driven to unfortunate measures by the arming of the Ulster Volunteers and the disappointment of his political hopes. Under these influences, so went the theory, he turned to Germany merely because Germany was then at war with England, and because he thought he might find among the Irish prisoners of war men who would range themselves on the side of the Irish Volunteers. The allegation that he ever sought to enlist Irish soldiers to fight against England was stoutly denied; all, it was protested, that he ever desired was to induce them, when the war was over, and if necessity unhappily arose, to enlist them to fight for Ireland. That ingenious theory vanished into thin air the moment it is examined in the light of Casement's career, and the activities on which he entered immediately upon his arrival in Ireland in 1903.

From an early period of his life Casement fell under German influence. He was associated with Mr Morel in the Congo atrocity agitation, a campaign doubtless humanitarian, but curiously subserving Germany's twofold purpose of generating ill-will between Belgium and Great Britain and of suggesting the blessedness of German Kultur as an alternative to Belgian barbarity. Casement was an ardent auxiliary to Mr Morel. British journalists, who were not reticent in their criticisms of Belgian rule, were surprised and bored by his haunting of newspaper offices and the way in which he urged them to more vigorous measures. (It was only after 1916 that his motives began to dawn upon them.) The allies of the Congo then parted, Morel to devote his energies to the development of German influence in Morocco, Casement to play a like part in relation to Ireland.

The connection between Casement and Germany, began in West Africa, became closer and more varied in succeeding years. His family was connected with Germany by marriage, he himself had business interests in that country, and was on very intimate relations with Germans in high positions, including Herr Ballin, the head of the Hamburg-Amerika line and a personal friend of the Kaiser, a very singular fact seeing that he was unacquainted with the German language.

One other point, and this brief review of Casement's antecedents may close. Holding the views he did, he accepted an offer of knighthood from the King with, it is said, some scruples of conscience. In his trial he found himself under the necessity of explaining his action, and did so by saying that he could not refuse. That statement was untrue. Both before and since his time men have respectfully declined similar offers. There is living a distiguished man of letters who declined an honour even after it had appeared in the *Gazette*. Casement did not decline, he accepted the offer in terms which have been euphemistically described as 'courtly,' but which would be more correctly described as servile. The language of his reply is the language of a man who, plotting treason, desired to disarm suspicion:

'I find it very hard to choose the words in which to make acknowledgment of the honour done me by the King. I am much moved at the proof of confidence and appreciation of my service on the Putumayo conveyed to me by your letter, wherein you tell me that the King had been graciously pleased upon your recommendation to confer upon me the honour of knighthood. I am, indeed, grateful to you for this signal assurance of your personal esteem and support. I am very deeply sensible of the honour done to me by His Majesty. I would beg that my humble duty might be presented to His Majesty when you may do me the honour to convey him my deep appreciation of the honour he has been so graciously pleased to confer upon me.'

And having written this letter we are informed that he never opened the parcel which contained the insignia.* If he were not then conscious of treason, why did he not even examine the symbol of the honour he had accepted with such abject gratitude? It may be a redeeming point in his moral character, but it is very suggestive of his political guilt. In that very year he was plotting with Professor Kuno Meyer, who was undoubtedly a German agent, to prevent a *rapprochement* between the United States and Great Britain and to embroil the relations between the two countries. He also wrote the first of a series of remarkable articles, entitled 'Ireland, Germany and the Freedom of the Seas,' to prove that Ireland's hope of freedom and the liberty of the world lay in alliance between Germany and Ireland to procure the downfall of the British Empire. These articles appeared in the *Gaelic American* after the outbreak of war, and will be referred to again later.

In 1913 Germany was making feverish, though secret, preparations for the great adventure. Twice during the preceding six years she had put out feelers in North Africa, to draw them in again when she found the ground not sufficiently prepared. Not all the efforts of Morel could convince the world that Morocco could only survive under the influence of Teutonic Kultur. Her path to world-empire lay elsewhere, and she was

* *The Irish Rebellion of* 1916, Wells and Marlowe.

getting ready for the journey while her agents and emissaries smoothed the way and blazed the trail. Just as in Belgium and France her engineers were secretly making concrete foundations for the big guns of 1914, so throughout the world her agents were puchasing spies and promoting disaffection among her potential foes. Her missionaries and consuls were busy in India, there were intrigues in South Africa, in every land under the British flag – for England was the enemy – spies were at their work. It was not likely that the Hun, thorough in all that was underhand, would omit so promising a sphere of operations as Ireland.

For Ireland was Great Britain's Achilles' heel, alike by her strategical position and the temper of her people. Philip of Spain, Louis of France, the Directory, all had been ready to use Irish disaffection against England, their enemy. In St Helena Napoleon lamented his failure to copy their example. 'Had I gone to Ireland instead of Egypt the Empire was at an end.' As it was in the sixteenth, seventeenth, and eighteenth centuries, so Germany meant that it should be in the twentieth, and Casement went to Ireland to fulfil the plan. It is possible that he desired to serve what he conceived to be Ireland's interests, but it is certain that he was anxious to serve the interests of Germany. During the year before the war in all the articles in the Sinn Fein papers that can be traced to his pen there is only one – and that a vile and filthy attack upon Lord Roberts – which is not concerned with Germany.

Almost immediately after his arrival in Ireland he opened his campaign with an article in the *Irish Review*, which has often been quoted, entitled 'Ireland, Germany and the Next War.' The article was signed 'Shan Van Vocht,' but there is no doubt that it was written by Casement. In this he discussed the thesis that it would be to Ireland's interest to support Great Britain in the event of a war because, were Britain defeated, she would either remain attached to England and so have to share the burden of defeat, or she would become the prey of the victor. 'Shan Van Vocht' rejected this thesis, pointing out that there was a third alternative – viz. that Ireland might be separated from Great Britain and established under European guarantees as a neutralised, independent European State.

'With Great Britain cut off and the Irish Sea held by German squadrons, no power from within could maintain any effective resistence to a German occupation of Dublin and a military occupation of the island. To convert that into a permanent administration could not be opposed from within, and, with Great Britain down and severed from Ireland by a victorious German Navy, it is obvious that opposition to the permanent retention of Ireland by the victor must come from within. It is equally obvious that it would come from without, and it is for this international reason that, I think, a permanent German annexation of any part of the United Kingdom need not be seriously feared. Such a complete change in the political geography of Europe as a German-owned Ireland could not but provoke universal alarm and a widespread combination to forbid its realisation.'

He then goes on to point out that Germany would have to attain her end, 'the permanent disabling of the maritime supremacy of Great Britain,' by the less provocative measure of establishing Ireland as a neutralised, independent State under international control. This he considered would be an arrangement that 'a Peace Congress should, in the end, be glad to ratify at the instance of a victorious Germany.'

Those who have read the works of General Bernhardi will realise how frail would have been that international combination on which Ireland was to depend for her independence. For Germany's plans did not contemplate the existence of any European Power that would be in any position to thwart or bend her purpose.

'Shan Van Vocht' admits that Germany would consult her own interests:

'That Germany should propose this form of dissolution in any interest but her own, or for the *beaux yeux* of Ireland, I do not for a moment assert.'

But he goes on to say that a neutralised Ireland would serve Germany's plans, while she would also be consulting the 'moral and intellectual' claims of Ireland. He sets forth his opinion in the following delicious sentence:

'Germany would attain her ends as the champion of National Liberty and could destroy England's naval supremacy for all time by an act of irreproachable morality.'

On such slender security as German morality was Ireland bidden to rally to 'the champion of National Liberty'. These are the words of a German agent enlisting recruits for his employer rather than of an Irish patriot enlisting an ally for his cause.

This article, which appeared in July, was sent to General Bernhardi by an anonymous correspondent – 't is not difficult to guess his identity – with a request that he should notice it. The General did so in September in the columns of the *Berliner Post:*

'Today, indeed, German policy seems to be steering full sail towards an arrangement with England, but as the goal could not be reached without the abandonment of our whole future as a world-Power, it is valuable for the *realpolitiker* to examine exhaustively both the strength and the weakness of England.'

He found signs of these 'weaknesses' in various parts of the world, such as India, Egypt and elsewhere, and then he continues:

'It is not without interest to know that, if it ever comes to a war with England, Germany will have allies in the enemy's camp itself, who in the given circumstances are resolved to bargain, and in any case will constitute a grave anxiety for England and perhaps tie fast a portion of the English troops. This is no time for Germany to pursue a policy of renunciation.'

General Bernhardi was duly rebuked by the official Press for his frankness, but 'Shan Van Vocht' had attained his purpose, and from that time forth the columns of *Irish Freedom*,* the organ of the Sinn Fein extremists and of Casement himself, teem with references to Germany as the saviour, and Ireland became the happy hunting ground of German Press correspondents and spies.

With all these Casement was in close relation. Especially would it seem that he was intimate with a certain Baron Von Horst, of the nature of whose mission in England there is no possible doubt. This man was of middle-class origin who had established a business in England, and who was ennobled for some mysterious reason, though indeed the mystery is not

* This paper was controlled by Macdermott and James Connolly. The former was a Sinn Feiner, so that this combination represented the alliance between the intellectual and proletarian movements. Both men were signatories to the Proclamation of the Irish Republic in 1916.

impenetrable in view of his operations. During his sojourn in England he developed a remarkable taste for British politics, and it is notable that his sympathies were invariably with those whose patriotism was dubious and whose desire to make trouble was evident. At one time he financed the *Herald*, which was being run by Mr George Lansbury, and over which every one who had touched it financially had burned his fingers. Undeterred by these painful examples, this benevolent foreigner found money for Mr Lansbury, and lost it. On the occasion of the dock strike, which resulted in the transfer of a good deal of trade from the Thames to the Elbe, the big-hearted Baron subscribed to the strike fund on a scale incommensurate with his means. Among his other enterprises he had a cinema theatre, which later became a meeting place for revolutionaries, or for any one likely to make trouble for the authorities. He also, some two months or so before the war, attempted to purchase rifles from a dealer in London, declaring himself to be the initiator of the Irish Volunteers. The deal, however, did not come off when his nationality was revealed. Baron Von Horst's career in Ireland finally terminated in August, 1914, when he was arrested for distributing anti-recruiting literature and interned.

In these and similar activities Baron Von Horst had the valuable assistance of a Miss Lillian Troy of California. When the Irish question threatened to develop into serious trouble, these inseparable comrades threw themselves into the fray, as always on the anti-British side. It was not long before the trio found a subject which by great good fortune served the double purpose of abusing England and of pointing to Germany as the appointed saviour of Ireland.

The Cunard Company gave notice of its intention to discontinue the practice of calling at Queenstown, in this doing just what the White Star Line had done previously. Casement at once made the heavens ring with his protests, and Baron Von Horst and Miss Troy joined in the chorus. The action of the company was only part of Britain's steadfast policy to injure Ireland's trade and to isolate her from the world. But it was a happy circumstance that Germany was animated by no such selfish purpose. The Hamburg-Amerika line would call at Queenstown and redress Ireland's wrong. Thus would England's machinations be defeated, and the visits of the German liners would link up Ireland with the continent of Europe, opening up new avenues of trade and vistas of prosperity. Miss Troy wrote in *Sinn Fein* an eulogium of the noble services of Von Horst and Casement, praising the energy with which the latter had pressed Ireland's case upon Herr Ballin, and extolling the skill and bravery of the German sailors in facing a harbour which English captains were afraid to enter. And then the Sinn Fein papers took up the tale, prompted no doubt by the ingenious operators of the scheme. The coming of the German liners, it was said, would lead to the establishment of close trade relations between Ireland and Germany. No longer would Ireland be compelled to sell her goods to England, her only customer, at an alarming sacrifice. Her cattle would cross the North Sea and fetch £2 a head more than they did in Liverpool and Bristol. No one explained, and indeed no one inquired why, if Germany wanted beef, she did not send to Ireland and get it where prices ruled so low; no one asked whether, as a fact, Germany needed to import cattle from oversea, or why England, which was searching every continent for food, and bringing livestock thousands of miles, should be able to buy Irish cattle so cheap. It was enough that England was being attacked, and Casement was happy enough to win great commendation from his countrymen and high credit from the foreigner whose cause he so ably served.

What may be called the 'Queenstown stunt' and the article in the *Irish Review* admirably prepared the way for that momentous step – the formation of the Irish Volunteers. From that moment Sinn Fein ceased to be a purely intellectual movement, and became an active revolutionary force.

There have been conflicting opinions as to motives which underlay the formation of the Irish Volunteers. The natural theory, and the one generally accepted at the time, was that they were to be used against the Ulster Volunteer Force. It may well be that some of those who enlisted cherished the same idea, and perhaps, like the Ribbonmen of some fifty years before, contemplated the possibility of wading in Orange-men's blood.

But these theories are wrong. Mr O'Hegarty is very emphatic in his denial of any intention to fight Ulster. 'They did not establish the Irish Volunteers as a counter-blast to the Ulster

Volunteers, or with any idea of either fighting or overawing Ulster.' The Ulster Volunteers counted for this much in the formation of their Southern rivals, – they encouraged those who wanted to have an armed force to make the attempt to form one. As the Government, so went the calculation, had permitted the Ulster-men to create a Volunteer force. 'there was a sporting chance' that it would not prohibit the formation of a similar body in the South of Ireland.* It may have been present to the minds of those who wished to arouse more bitter feelings against England that such a prohibition would admirably serve their purpose. As a fact Sinn Fein was disposed to be grateful for the opportunity. In the Manifesto of November 25th, 1913, which called for Volunteers, the conditions created by the Ulster movement were described at 'not altogether unfortunate'. The Manifesto also contained words which show that the real object of the promoters was not temporary action in reference to the Home Rule Bill, but something more far-reaching. 'The Volunteers, once they have been enrolled, will form a permanent element in the national life under a National Government.' When it is remembered that the Home Rule Bill, for which Mr Redmond was then battling, particularly prohibited the maintenance of armed forces by the Irish Government, this sentence is significant. It becomes perfectly clear that the kind of National Government which the Irish Volunteers were to serve was not the kind of National Government which the British would be at all likely to grant.

Among the founders of the Irish Volunteers there were moderate men, who never contemplated, and would have shrunk in abhorrence from anything revolutionary. There always are such moderate men in revolutionary enterprises, men whose moderation makes them useful auxiliaries outside, but whose moderation excludes them from the inner council. They think they are leaders, while really they are only decoys. One of them, Col. Moore, formerly of the Connaught Rangers, in later days described the *personnel* of the original Committee, of about twenty-five. It took him two or three days 'to size them up and separate the groups.' And he thus described them:

'There were about two extremists and four of five boys under their domination. . . . Five or six Sinn Feiners were in a

* O'Hegarty, *Sinn Fein.*

separate group; they might be described as extreme Home Rulers; they did not approve of the methods of the Parliamentary Party, but were not revolutionists. There were a few like MacNeill, Pearse, Macdonagh, Plunkett and O'Rahilly, who belonged to no especial political party; they were Idealists. The remainder of the Committee were moderate men, inclined to follow the Parliamentary Party.'*

Col. Moore says in his letter that it is interesting to note how some of the Sinn Feiners and Idealists gradually became extremists and merged with the Fenians. The process of evolution was not gradual, but rapid, so rapid that it is more than doubtful if there were any evolution at all. It is infinitely more probable that whatever there was of evolution in their political principles had already been accomplished when Col. Moore met them, and that they already had their goal in view, though they kept it concealed from their moderate colleagues. For of the five idealists whom he names four took part in the Rebellion: Professor MacNeill was only deterred from doing so by the arrest of Casement and the capture of the Aud.

Very significant of the real nature and aims of the Volunteer movement is the effect it had upon the fortunes of Sinn Fein. As we have seen, it had been a year before in abject poverty. It had never been well off. Mr Hegarty states that one contested election, involving an expenditure of, at the outside, £1000, had seriously crippled it. But now it bounded into affluence, and the money came from the Clan-na-Gael, which had long been watching its developments and was now assured that it was on the right line. Pearse, who was one of the original Committee, had, like the Countess Markievics, one foot in Connolly's Labour Movement and the other in Sinn Fein, and Connolly and Larkin were favourably known to the extremists of America as revolutionaries of the most approved brand. It is impossible to doubt that the true motive of the Irish Volunteers was revolutionary, though it is possible that the revolutionary tendencies were further quickened by the insistence of the trans-Atlantic paymaster.

It is extremely instructive to read the fuller-blooded Sinn Fein journals at this period. *Sinn Fein* itself, Mr Arthur Griffith's organ, remains more or less intellectual and economic in its

* Col. Moore, *Freeman's Journal*, May 30th, 1916.

outlook. *Irish Freedom,* the channel through which Casement addressed the public, was more outspoken. Mr Daly weekly regaled its readers with his Fenian reminiscences; essays on military tactics filled columns. But, perhaps most remarkable of all, was the sudden revival of the Wolfe Tone cult, which was coincident with the formation of the Volunteer Force. When we remember that Wolfe Tone's two claims to his country's gratitude were that he had organised a rebellion at the time when Ireland had her own Parliament, and had called in foreign allies to aid him in his purpose of destroying Grattan's Parliament as an engine of British tyranny, this sudden and passionate revival of his memory is not a little suggestive – suggestive not only of the aims of the inner circle, but of the means by which they were to be attained.

CHAPTER X

ARMS AND THE MAN

Grant us a great war for the liberty of the peoples,
We pray Thee, O Lord.
For arms and our flag raised again in battle,
We pray Thee, O Lord.

WITH a litany, from which the above is an extract, did *Irish Freedom* hail the opening of 1914, the year of Fate.

It is curious how this idea of war runs like a scarlet thread through all the articles in *Irish Freedom* at this period; it would be surprising, were it not certain that Casement's was the mind which inspired, and his often the hand that wrote them. The world was not thinking of war. Such uneasiness as existed when the Kaiser made his theatrical *démarche* at Agadir had faded out of mind; the war in the Balkans, the powder magazine of Europe, had produced no explosion. Lord Haldane had brought back a cheery optimism from Berlin, and no one knew that it was assumed; at the very moment when the Sinn Fein paper was publishing its grim litany the British Chancellor was assuring the country that never was the time more opportune for reducing the vote for armaments. The Chanceries of Europe might be vigilant, but the people were careless, working and playing as they worked and played in Pompeii the day before the dead volcano awoke to new life. The only thought of war in England was when men prayed for peace in their time. But in Ireland men were talking war, thinking war. praying for war, because Casement taught them – and Casement knew.

Up to this moment he had played his part with patience. He had, indeed, been active when Germany made her tentative move in Morocco in 1911. His visits to Ireland then were frequent, his confabulations with Kuno Meyer constant. Though the necessity for action then had passed away, his time had not been wasted, for he had made friendships and preparations which stood him in good stead two years later. In the interval he had acquired a title and gained a reputation which helped him nicely, and his retirement from the service was fortunately coincident with an emergency which would demand his unfettered services. So in 1913 he could gather together all the strings, and play his secret part in forming the Irish Volunteers, not merely to counteract the Ulster movement or to win Ireland's freedom, but to assist in keeping those British troops at home which General Bernhardi regarded as of such first-rate importance.

It is very notable how Casement's activities increased as the months went on. He may not have known that in August of 1913 Germany had actually informed Italy of her intention to make war on Serbia, and had only held her hand when Italy declined to take a part in the game. But he knew, as every German agent knew, that the Day was near at hand, and that this time there would be no drawing back.

There appeared in *Irish Freedom* for March, 1914, an article which can with the utmost certainty be ascribed to Casement. It is signed 'The Poor Old Woman'. Now, this is the English translation of 'Shan Van Vocht,' the *nom de plume* of the writer of the article in the *Irish Review* quoted in the previous chapter. There is, moreover, in the article a most remarkable illustration of Great Britain's method of dealing with her subject nationalities. She is compared to the 'Sipo Matador,' or 'murdering creeper' of Brazil. If we remember that Casement was 'Shan Van Vocht,' that he was Consul-General in Brazil and was familiar with its forest life from his experiences at Putumayo, we may adapt the words of Macaulay when he fixed the authorship of Junius's letters on Sir Philip Francis, and say, 'Either Casement or the Devil'.

The article commences with these remarkable words:

'In these opening days of 1914 I bring with a message of hope, these scattered thoughts upon the British Empire and its approaching dissolution to lay before the youth of Ireland. I say dissolution advisedly. . . . Home Rule will not save it. The attempt to bribe Ireland, and the greater Ireland beyond the seas . . . will not suffice. The issue lies in stronger hands.'

He then draws the parallel above mentioned between Britain

and the 'Sipo Matador,' and continues: 'A brave hand may yet cut the "Sipo Matador," and the slayer be slain before he has quite stifled his victim.' Then follows a lurid picture of the complacent security of the Empire and its approaching doom.

'"All's well with God's world" – and poet and plagiarist, courtier and courtesan, Kipling and cant – these now dally by the banks of the Thames and dine off the peoples of the earth, just as once the degenerate populace of Imperial Rome fed upon the people of the pyramids. But the end is near at hand. The "Secret of Empire" is no longer the sole possession of England. Other people are learning to think imperially. *The Goths and Visigoths of modern Europe are upon the horizon. . . . London, like Rome, will have strange guests. They will not pay their hotel bills.*'

And finally Casement denounces England's attempt to 'bribe' America by giving Ireland Home Rule:

'*Were the Anglo-Saxon alliance ever consummated it would be the biggest crime in human history.* . . . The emanations of Thames sewage are all over the world, and the sewers are running still. The penalty for the pollution of the Thames is a high one, but the prize for the pollution of the Mississippi is higher still. . . . *The "Anglo-Saxon" Alliance means a compact to ensure slavery and to beget war.* . . . The true alliance to aim at for all who love peace is the friendly union of Germany, America, and Ireland.These are the true United States of the World. Ireland, the link between Germany and America, must be freed by both.'*

We need not pause to consider the view which Casement takes of an Anglo-Saxon alliance, though Americans may be astonished to learn that it only needs their co-operation with the people from whom they sprang to rivet the chains of slavery upon a world devastated by wanton war. Nor need we waste time over American sensations when this discovery comes to their notice. The really significant point is that Casement represents Germany as the only humanising factor in any world-ruling alliance. And in this alliance Ireland is to be a partner. This is an advance on the position of a neutralised State assigned to her in the *Irish Review* article. She is now to be the link

* *Irish Freedom*, March, 1914. The italics are ours.

between the two World States, America and Germany; they three are to be the true United States of the World.

After such an outpouring can it be doubted that the Irish Volunteers were to be something more than a Fenian Brotherhood, that they were to be the pledge of Ireland's fidelity to the Kaiser? Many of the Volunteer leaders did not know it; Professor John MacNeill, Gaelic Leaguer and idealist, did not realise at that time that he was not an apostle but a dupe, not a leader but a fraudulent advertisement. He realised it later, but he was then too enmeshed to secape from the net.

This scheme was planned and executed by one who had accepted honours and was at that moment receiving a pension from the British Government. A few months later this same man wrote in *Fianna* an article which *Irish Freedom* declared was delightful and indispensable to every Irish boy. It was on the subject of 'Chivalry'.

Its author was at that time, July, 1914, in America, whither he had been sent to act as liaison officer between the American Irish extremists and the German Government. But before he went he wrote, or inspired, a final appeal to the Irish people. It was headed 'Arm Quickly.' A few extracts will show its nature:

'Again the events of this past few months have restored Ireland to international status. Since the mission of Wolfe Tone to Paris Europe has forgotten Ireland and has never given a thought to the possible importance of Ireland in the conflict of European interests. . . . Ireland is again coming to be a factor in the thoughts and plans and life of Europe. . . . For Ireland the tide has turned and is running with an almost fearful swiftness. . . . *Stranger events than any that have come yet may come very soon, and probably will come*. . . . There is one urgent duty that devolves upon every Irishman at this moment, more urgent than any other. . . . That duty is to become armed, and to become armed very quickly.'*

If Casement's forecast of the ending of the great war was mistaken, how marvellously prophetic was he of its coming! Within three months the Austrian Archduke died in Serajevo, within four Germany had launched her ultimatum. Even in minor details his prophecies were fulfilled. Strange visitors,

* *Irish Freedom*, May, 1914. The italics are ours.

Goths and Visigoths, visited London. They did not pay their hotel bills. And Casement himself was one of them.

About this time the conspirators began to separate, each betaking himself to his appointed task. The preliminary work was done. Kuno Meyer and Casement had striven to block that Anglo-Saxon alliance which would have opposed so terrible a barrier to Teutonic ambition, they had contrived to turn the eyes of Ireland to Germany as her liberator, as in former days they had turned to Spain and France. And this they had done, not only to secure liberty for Ireland, but to secure the Empire of the World for Germany. Casement probably thought primarily of the first of these objects as Kuno Meyer would naturally think most of the second, and so they made their bargain. Before he wrote 'Ireland and the Next War' or 'The Elsewhere Empire,' from which we have just quoted, Casement had written an article, 'The Keeper of the Seas,' which was published in August, 1911. Its general tenor is the same, but there are a few sentences which deserve quotation, as refuting once and for all the theory that the Irish Volunteers were formed to counterbalance the Volunteers of Ulster, or that the present movement is due to dissatisfaction with the Home Rule Bill or discontent at its postponement. The article also affords food for thought to those who contemplate measures tending to weaken the connection between Great Britain and Ireland. Casement's words may yet be heard on many platforms.

'Without Ireland there would be today no British Empire. The vital importance of Ireland to England is understood but never proclaimed by every British statesman . . . and the vital importance of Ireland to Europe is not, and has not been, understood by any European statesman. To them it has not been a European island, a vital and necessary element of European development, but an appanage of England, an island beyond an island. Montesquieu alone of French writers grasped the importance of Ireland in the international affairs of his time; and he blames the vacillation of Louis XIV., who failed to put forth his strength to establish James upon the throne of Ireland, and thus by an act of perpetual separation to "*affaiblir le voisin.*' Napoleon, too late in St Helena, realised his error: "Had I gone to Ireland instead of Egypt, the Empire of England was at an end." Perhaps the one latter-day European who perceived the true relation of Ireland to England was Niebuhr. "Should England," he said. "not change her conduct, Ireland may still, for a long period, belong to her, but not always; and the loss of that country is the death-day, not only of her greatness, but of her very existence.' . . . Detach Ireland from the map of the British Empire and restore it to the map of Europe and that day England resumes her native proportions and Europe assumes its rightful stature in the Empire of the World. Ireland can only be restored to the current of European life, from which she has for so long been purposely withheld, by the act of Europe. What Napolean perceived too late may yet be the purpose and achievement of a Congress of Nations. . . . Ireland's strategic importance is a factor of supreme weight to Europe, and is today used in the scale against Europe. . . . The *arbitrium mundi,* claimed and most certainly exercised by England, is maintained by the British fleet; and until that power is effectively challenged and held in check, it is idle to talk of European influence outside of certain narrow Continental limits. The power of the British Fleet can never be permanently restrained until Ireland is restored to Europe.'

This constant reiteration of the word 'Europe' is, of course, the merest *camouflage,* to use the expression of the day. How could 'Europe' resume its rightful stature in the Empire of the World? Individual nations have held their place in world-empire, but never a Continent. If Europe had felt the pressure of Britain's fleets of United Europe that of Great Britain would be powerless. The late war taught us how difficult, even with vast naval supremacy, and in alliance with France and Italy, the problem of living could become. For 'Europe' then we must read some other name, and that Casement and Kuno Meyer supply in their concluding sentence:

'Germany then of necessity becomes the champion of European interests as opposed to the world-dominion of England.'

And poor, blind, besotted Europe never saw it!

'In the summer of 1914, then, the friends separated, Kuno Meyer to go to Germany, Casement to America. But, before he sailed, he went to London – he himself told the story in a New York paper – where he made final arrangements with a small band of Irish friends, whom he had gathered together in May, 1914, to purchase arms on the Continent and to land them in Ireland. He does not say what these arrangements were, but it is a fact that about that time there began to appear in the *Gaelic American,* an extreme Clan-na-Gael paper, a series of lengthy articles contributed by Lieut.-Col. J. T. Warburton, formerly of the Royal Engineers, who referred in them to his connection with Casement. These articles were calculated to give great comfort and satisfaction to the clients of the *Gaelic American.* They contained grossly vulgar references to the Queen, violent diatribes against Mr Redmond, and the coarsest abuse of the service to which Col. Warburton had once belonged. British soldiers, said Col. Warburton, were 'justly described by the New York Volunteer Committee as the laughing-stock of soldiers throughout the world.' They had shown cowardice in the New Zealand War, where he himself had fought; the Boers had 'kicked them from one end of South Africa to another'; if an expedition were sent to France (this in August, 1914), 'I expect it will soon be defeated and surrender.' 'The British Army,' he wrote, 'is a negligible quantity, because it contains but few Irish and Scots.' He rejoiced greatly during the retreat from Mons – 'The British have bolted and have been driven like sheep before the Germans.' Their flight was disgraceful because their casualties had not been heavy, and he hints not obscurely that officers were voluntarily surrendering themselves. The English had no military ardour – 'We are tremedously martial so long as there is no fighting.' As for Kitchener's Army, it was hopeless. Public-houses had to be closed at 11 p.m. because the men got drunk, and Kitchener himself did not know what to do with them. And in the *Gaelic American* of August 22nd he makes this impassioned appeal:

'Are our American friends prepared to send rifles to help England against a country which has never harmed her? I think not.'

In all that has been written about the Great War the patriotic efforts of this fine British soldier, probably drawing a pension, have received no mention. But they should not pass unrecorded.

Having set these forces at work, Casement went to America, and on August 1st he was staying in Philadelphia with Mr Joseph McGarrity. The nature of his business with Mr Mc-

Garrity may be judged from a telegram sent by the German Foreign Office to Count von Bernstorff, the German Ambassador at Washington, on January 26th, 1916:–

'January 26, for Military Attaché. You can obtain particulars as to persons suitable for carrying on sabotage in the United States and Canada from the following persons: (1) Joseph M'Garrity, Philadelphia, Pa.; (2) John P. Kealing, Michigan Avenue, Chicago; (3) Jeremiah O'Leary, 16, Park Row, New York. One and two are absolutely reliable, but not always discreet. These persons are indicated by Sir Roger Casement. In the United States sabotage can be carried out on every kind of factory for supplying munitions of war. Railway embankments and bridges must not be touched. Embassy must in no circumstances be compromised. Similar precautions must be taken in regard to Irish pro-German propaganda.

'Signed, Representative of General Staff.'*

It is melancholy to have to record that the discreet Mr Jeremiah O'Leary was, in June, 1918, indicted, together with John Ryan, an attorney in Buffalo, Lieut.-Commander Wessels, of the German Navy, and Baroness Maria von Kretschmann, a relative of the German Empress, for acts of treason, such as giving military information, destruction of piers, docks and troop transports with bombs, assisting Germany in landing an armed expedition in Ireland, fomenting a revolt in Ireland, and so on.

On August 22nd there appeared in the *Gaelic American* the first of a series of six articles by Casement, under the title of 'Ireland, Germany and the Freedom of the Seas.' Part I., he said, was written in 1911, and the other five at odd moments between that time and 1913. The first of the series was written before the Home Rule Bill was drawn, and therefore represented a settled policy formulated without regard to the merits of that measure, while all six were written while the author was a high official in the service of Great Britain, accepting knighthood with fulsome professions of gratitude. In them Casement elaborates the doctrines already described, but he brings them up-to-date with a few sentences which may be quoted:

* Published by American Government.

'England fights as the foe of Europe and the enemy of civilisation. In order to destroy German shipping, German commerce, German industry, she has deliberately planned the conspiracy we now see at work. The war of 1914 is England's war. . . . The crippling of the British fleet will mean a joint German-Irish invasion of Ireland.'

And then Casement ceases from his literary propaganda with the remark: 'The rest of the writer's work must be essayed not with the author's pen, but with the rifle of the Irish Volunteer.'

By this time Sinn Fein had completely abandoned any pretence of moderation. Professor MacNeill was writing impassioned appeals to Mr Joseph M'Garrity for arms. 'We entreat and beseech you to join with us, making this the grand effort of our lives, and shrinking from no sacrifice that the peril and the hope of so great a crisis may demand.'* Mr Arthur Griffith, who, though he numbered Sir Roger Casement among the contributors to his paper *Sinn Fein,* had managed to preserve an appearance of decent moderation so long as it paid, allowed his real self to appear when war broke out.

'Ireland is not at war with Germany. She has no quarrel with any Continental power. . . . England is at war with Germany. Germany is nothing to us in herself, but she is not an enemy.'†

A little later Mr Griffith had an opportunity to help Germany and he eagerly seized it. Casement wrote two letters to Ireland from America, one of which was stopped by the British Censorship, while the other got through. In it Casement begged Irishmen to stay at home, and to refuse to assist England in her dishonest attack on a people with whom Ireland had no ground of quarrel. This letter was published in *Sinn Fein* at great length and, in an abbreviated form, in the *Irish Independent,* and had an immediate effect in stopping recruiting. In order to clinch the matter, Casement, to quote his own words, 'hoped that the German Government might be induced to make clear its peaceful intention towards Ireland, and that the effect of such a pronouncement in Ireland itself might be powerful enough to keep Irishmen from volunteering for a war that had no claim upon their patriotism or their honour. With this aim

* *Gaelic American*, July 18th, 1914.

† *Sinn Fein*, August 8th, 1914.

chiefly in view I came to Germany in November, 1914, and I succeeded in my purpose. "The German Government declared openly its goodwill to Ireland and in convincing terms".'

Here we touch an extremely important point. During the latter part of 1918, and in this present year, *Sinn Fein* has discovered that it had backed the wrong horse and has been trying to hedge. Its leaders, except the impulsive Countess Markievics, have repeatedly declared that there was no alliance with Germany. They have further declared – Mr De Valera has done so repeatedly in America – that they never received any German money.* Both these statements are absolute and deliberate falsehoods, and this is a convenient place to consider them.

And first as to the alliance. The 'convincing terms' in which Germany expressed her goodwill to Ireland were sent to America by wireless and published in November 21st, 1914:

'Sir Roger Casement was received at the Foreign Office and pointed out statements which have appeared in Ireland . . . that German victory would inflict great loss on the Irish people. In reply the Acting Secretary of State of the Foreign Office, by order of the Imperial Chancellor, officially declared that the German Government repudiated the evil intentions attributed to it, and only desires the welfare of the Irish people and country. Germany would never invade Ireland with a view to its conquest or the overthrow of any native institutions of that country. Should fortune ever bring German troops to Ireland's shores they would land there, not as an army of invaders to pillage and destroy, but as forces of a nation inspired by goodwill towards the country and people for whom Germany desires only national prosperity and freedom.'

The view taken of this document by the American-Irish is evident from the following resolution adopted by the New York Irish Volunteer Fund Committee:–

'No honest friend of the Irish people would assail a man who secured such a guarantee from a friendly Power as Sir Roger Casement has secured from the Government of the German Empire, a guarantee which will remove any doubt which may

* See *Irish Independent*, July 17th, 1919. Mr De Valera's words are, 'I have denied time and again that our organisation has received a mark or a rouble, and call on those who make the charges to substantiate them.'

have been entertained regarding German goodwill by a section of the Irish People.' *

But Germany did not give this friendly guarantee for nothing. The contract had to be bilateral. The inducement held out by Casement that such a guarantee would keep Irishmen from enlisting was well enough, but it would be more to the purpose were Irishmen to exchange that attitude of passive neutrality for one of active co-operation. Casement readily fell in with the idea, if indeed he had not already conceived it. Very probably he was delighted to get such easy terms. It is extremely curious to observe how his intercourse with the Germans had caused him to absorb their peculiar mentality which enables them to ignore any point of view except their own, and to invert with a garb of virtue anything that makes for their advantage. Some eight months later, August 7th, 1915, Casement wrote a letter, which was published in the *Gaelic American*, in which he described his experiences among the Irish prisoners. He repudiated as a 'stupid and childish lie' Mr Redmond's assertion that he had been mobbed by the soldiers whom he had endeavoured to enlist for his Irish Brigade. He had, he said, walked among them alone and unguarded. It was indeed true that some of the 'silly youths' had declared that 'they were Englishmen and had no use for an Irish traitor'. But he goes on, 'I paid no attention to these valiant supporters of Mr Redmond. . . . Had those friends of Mr Redmond been as brave in body as they were in words, I might have had to use my cane'. And he concludes this astonishing epistle: 'All the Irish prisoners of war at Limburg are not renegades and corner boys, but then all of them are not followers of Mr Redmond and fighting for British ideals of civilisation, progress, and humanity.'

It must have been a shock to him to find that out of two thousand five hundred men only fifty-two responded to his seduction. Having himself found it so easy to conspire against the country whose pay and rewards he was taking, he must have been amazed to find among these poor half-starved, ill-used, poorly paid 'Tommies' such loyalty to the King to whom they had sworn fealty. In his distress he resolved to call religion to his aid. He sent a message to his friends in America through

* *Gaelic American*, December 5th, 1914.

Count Bernstorff, the German Foreign Office acting as intermediary, asking them to send a priest to help him, and in responce they despatched a certain Father Nicholson, whose efforts were no more successful.*

Such was the bargain, made and kept by both the contracting parties. If ever in this world there was an alliance, that between Sinn Fein and Germany was one.

Now as to the question of the receipt of German money by Sinn Fein. As might be expected, these financial transactions were carried out with every precaution to obey the instructions of the German Foreign Office that the Embassy at Washington was not to be compromised. Revelations made at a later date by the American Government show that moneys paid from that source flowed through most tortuous channels, so that, like the victims of the U-boats, it should 'leave no trace'. But in spite of these precautions there is full knowledge of financial transactions between Count Bernstorff and the American directors of the Irish movement, including Mr John Devoy, the editor of the *Gaelic American*. The terms of the treaty made by Casement were printed in Berlin in a leaflet which was circulated in Ireland as coming from the German Foreign Office. But this is not all. We have Count Bernstorff's own words to prove the allegations.

After the failure of the Dublin rebellion Sinn Fein found itself in low water. Its desire for revolution was undiminished, but its purse was empty. In these circumstances it appealed to Count Bernstorff for help, in itself an indication that it had made similar appeals before. On June 17th, 1916, the Foreign Office informed Count Bernstorff that help would be forthcoming if Sinn Fein would indicate what was wanted. In July Count Bernstorff replied to Berlin. Things, he said, were moving again in Ireland and the rebels were reorganising their forces. They were, he added, in need of money, but he had put that matter right.

This revelation is doubly interesting, first because it proves beyond contradiction that Sinn Fein did receive German money; next because it destroys the fiction, concocted by some

* Trial of Joseph Dowling, *Times*, July 9th, 1918. See also Report of Casement's trial.

Though in Ireland party passion did not reach such heights of expression, it was rising every day, fanned by the news of the Irish-German alliance, which arrived through wireless stations, of which, as Count Bernstorff informed Berlin, there were many in Ireland.* The terms of the German statement were printed in Berlin in leaflet form and were circulated in the country. Large numbers of this leaflet, as well as of Casement's articles on 'Ireland, Germany and the Freedom of the Seas,' were found, together with ammunition and explosives, in the house of a man called De Lacy at Enniscorthy, County Wexford, in February.† Proclamations were posted up in many parts of the county to the following effect:

'People of Wexford.

'Take no notice of the police order to destroy your property and leave your homes if a German Army lands in Ireland. When the Germans come they will come as friends and put an end to English rule in Ireland. Therefore, stay in your homes, and assist as far as possible the German troops. Any stores, hay, corn, or forage taken by the Germans will be paid for by them.'

German agents and spies were ubiquitous and busy at this time. Baron Von Horst was arrested for distributing anti-recruiting and seditious literature; Lody, a greater than he, was captured at Killarney, where, it was stated before the Rebellion Commission, one of the hotel waiters was also a German spy. Up and down the country agents were at work, predicting British defeat and extolling the single-minded generosity of the Huns. Stories were current in the west of Ireland which illustrate the effect of these efforts, among them the following, which is within the knowledge of the writer. A vessel, it was said, had been stopped by a U-boat off the south-west coast. When the German commander learned that she was carrying grain to an Irish port, he bade her proceed. 'I will never,' he handsomely declared, 'interfere with the food of the priests and good people of Ireland.'

The disposition of the conspirators in 1915 was as follows: In

* Government statement, May 25th, 1918.

† Enniscorthy was one of the centres of rebellion in 1916. De Lacy escaped to America, where he intrigued with German agents and was given two years' imprisonment.

Germany Casement was making desperate efforts to make good his pledge to the German Government; in America Kuno Meyer was stumping the country, ostensibly lecturing on the Gaelic language, but really carrying on intrigues the nature of which may be easily defined, while leaders such as John Devoy, Judge Cohalan, and Jeremiah O'Leary, directed operations, and Count Bernstorff obligingly violated the cannons of diplomatic usage by allowing them to use his post-bag, and acted as paymaster. Of the American-Irish John Devoy was the most active and trusted agent. There was even a secret code, the 'Cypher Devoy,' which was specially used for communications between the rebels and their German allies.* In Ireland the Sinn Fein leaders denounced the Constitutional Nationalists, extolled Germany, vilified every Irishman who donned the British uniform, with special terms of reproach for any who, like Corporal O'Leary, might have earned particular glory, and worked feverishly on the task of drilling and equipping the Volunteers. They had their reward in later days, when Professor Edouard Meyer of the University of Berlin declared that 'during the war Ireland had shown herself Germany's true ally, not only with arms in her hands, but by her passive resistance.'

The sinking of the *Lusitania,* though it was hailed with delight by the American conspirators, caused them much embarrassment. Prior to that event, though they had grumbled openly at what they regarded as President Wilson's one-sided neutrality, they clung to the belief that a large section of the American people were friendly to Germany, or at least strictly impartial in their sentiments, After the atrocity that fond hope vanished. The German Empire sank with the great ship: the same torpedo destroyed both. All semblance of sympathy for the Central Empires disappeared, and it needed the firm hand of the President to hold his people back. America did not enter the war until two years later, it is true, but the altered sentiments of the nation must have been disconcerting to Devoy and his colleagues, and may possibly have had some effect in precipitating events in Ireland. The change in American feeling and its influence on the Sinn Fein leaders may be traced in the editorials of the *Gaelic American,* in the added virulence of

* Von Igel papers. Published by the American Committee of Public Safety, September 23rd, 1917.

their attacks on the American papers, and the steadily growing list of journals that came under their ban.

In Ireland things began to move swiftly as the year went on. Organisers formed new detachments of Volunteers throughout the southern provinces and the numbers were steadily swelled by desertions from the National Volunteers. Arms were smuggled in, including some machine guns; weapons were stolen from the National Volunteers, and were obtained by thefts or purchase from soldiers home on leave; explosives were concealed in convenient places and bombs were manufactured. Old soldiers acted as instructors, and the Sinn Fein papers devoted much of their space to articles on military tactics, such as street fighting, defence or destruction of roads and bridges, rearguard actions, and such modifications of established rules as were necessitated by the nature of the country. Germany helped with very full instructions in staff work, and with admirable maps of Dublin and the country.

The most important event of this period, however, was the alliance that was formed between the Irish Volunteers and the Citizen Army, important less from the strictly military point of view than from its ultimate political results. As a fighting force the Citizen Army was almost negligible; it added some hundreds of desperate men, mainly concentrated in Dublin to the Irish Volunteers, and indeed it was the Citizen Army which was most effective in the Dublin rebellion. But the junction between the forces had enormous political consequences. It brought together the two revolutionary currents, thenceforth to flow in a single stream. Except for a few idealists like Pearse, Sinn Fein had scant sympathy with the economic aims of Connolly and Larkin – Arthur Griffith, indeed, was strongly opposed to the great Dublin strike. Larkin and Connolly, on their side, would regard the responsible Sinn Feiners, such as Count Plunkett, Professor MacNeill, Mr Sweetman, and The O'Rahilly, as natural enemies. They found a link of union in hatred of Great Britain, and thenceforward the national movement changed its character. As always happens in revolutions, so soon as the intellectuals call the *sans culottes* to their aid, they become merged in the proletarian movement. Up to 1915 Great Britain had to deal with a political and intellectual movement: since that time, and now, she is faced by a revolutionary force no longer wholly political, but infused and largely inspired by anarchical doctrines. Thus Sinn Fein saddled itself with an incubus, fatal to its original principles, and destined to be embarrassing in the lst degree. The day will surely come when, like Mr Bumble, it will bitterly lament that it sold its liberty so cheap.

With the opening of 1916 the Irish leaders determined that the 'Day' had arrived. Those in America probably found their position getting more irksome. An American writer has said: 'If Americans had small patience with Ulster in 1914, they had still less with Sinn Fein in 1916.'* Casement, in Berlin, was being pressed by Germany to deliver the goods'. His failure to seduce the Irish soldiers had somewhat shaken Teutonic faith in his reliability, and he had to do something to redeem his promises. In Ireland the conspirators had prepared elaborate and, on paper, extremely effective plans of campaign; they probably calculated too optimistically the amount of aid that Germany would lend; moreover, though Mr Birrell refused to be alarmed, their spies in the Government Departments reported that other officials were awakening to a sense of realities; and so they resolved that the time had come to strike.

During March, 1916, messages were going back and forward between Germany and America, as to the transmission of arms to Tralee Bay, the possibility of U-boats entering the Liffey, and arranging a code of signals for use during these operations. The Irish Volunteers carried out a few dress rehearsals in Dublin, including a sham attack on the Castle, and Professor MacNeill, as Chief of Staff, ordered general marches and parades of the Volunteers for Easter Sunday, April 23rd.

On April 18th, the following despatch was sent to Count Bernstorff, marked 'very secret':

'Judge Cohalan requests the transmission of the following remarks: The revolution in Ireland can only be successful with the support of Germany; otherwise England will be able to suppress it, even though it be only after a hard struggle. Therefore help is necessary. This should consist principally of aerial attacks on England and a diversion of the fleet simultaneously with the Irish revolution. Then if possible a landing of arms and ammunition in Ireland and possibly some officers from

* Waldo G. Leland, *Quarterly Review*, July, 1918.

Zeppelins. This would enable the Irish ports to be closed against England and the cutting of the food supply for England. The services of the revolution, therefore, may decide the war.'*

The rest is known. On April 21st, the *Aud* was sighted by the *Bluebell*. She professed to be a Norwegian ship, bound from Bergen to Genoa. Dissatisfied and suspicious, the commander of the *Bluebell* ordered her to accompany him to Queenstown. On the morning of the following day the *Aud* hoisted German colours, the crew took to the boats and the vessel soon afterwards sank. She was manned by German officers and sailors, and carried a large cargo of arms and ammunition. On the 21st, too, Casement, with two companions, landed from a German submarine at Curraghgane, in Tralee Bay, and was arrested within a few hours. The news reached Professor MacNeill on Saturday, and he issued orders cancelling the marches and parades on the following day. He was willing to wound, but, in face of Casement's arrest and the failure of the German munitions to reach Ireland, he was too prudent to strike. Others did strike, but the plans had gone awry, and the rebellion was crushed. But for an accident to a motor-car, it would not have been crushed in a week, on such small chances do great matters hinge. Had the car met Casement, Professor MacNeill would have been less prudent, his volunteers would have gone out for their manœuvers, provisioned for a few days' bivouac.† As it was, the revolution was mainly confined to Dublin, though there was fighting also in Galway, Wexford, and County Dublin, where two officers and eight men of the Royal Irish Constabulary were killed and fourteen wounded, while in Tralee the Volunteers were mobilised. The sinking of the *Aud* and the arrest of Casement did not prevent a calamity, but they averted a very grave danger.

So Casement passed from the stage, the most ignoble of all the leading players in the drama.

The loss of life – of material damage to Dublin we say nothing – was not inconsiderable. Of those who fought for the Crown, 19 officers and 109 of other ranks were killed, and 46 officers and 326 other ranks were wounded. From the hospitals

* Found by American Secret Service agents in the office of Von Igel, a German agent. *New York World*, Sept. 23rd, 1817.

† *Irish Volunteer*, April 22nd, 1916.

180 civilians were reported killed and 614 wounded, and this certainly does not exhaust the list of casualties.

For a country which is uniformly described in Ireland as revelling in tyranny, the retribution exacted by Great Britain was not excessive. Some three thousand rebels were arrested, two thousand of whom were deported, the great majority being released in a few months. Of the leaders, fifteen were executed. Others, sentenced to death, had their sentences commuted to penal servitude for life, but were all released in a little more than a year. Among them was De Valera, who commanded one of the rebel detachments in Dublin, and who was among the last to surrender. Thus, by midsummer 1917 not a single rebel remained in prison for offences connected with the rising, and only fifteen of those who had hatched the plot which caused such ruin and suffering had paid the extreme penalty.

Nevertheless the epithets applied to General Maxwell, the Commander-in-Chief, would have been more appropriate, if indeed not excessive, if applied to Wallenstein or Alva. The Bishop of Limerick, being restrained by his episcopal position, contented himself with writing to the Guardians of the Tipperary Union of 'that brute Maxwell, who in my opinion is only one degree less objectionable than the Government that screens behind him'. What he might have said had he been a mere layman is interesting as a speculation, but must be neglected in view of the succeeding portion of the letter, which is not only interesting, but important, since it gave the cue for the future Irish policy:

'Ireland is not dead yet. While her young men are not afraid to die for her in open fight; and when defeated stand proudly with their backs to the wall as targets for English bullets, we need not despair of the old land.'*

This pronouncement had all the more effect because the Bishop had generally been regarded as a moderate, exercising a conservative influence upon Nationalist thought. Its immediate result was to unmuzzle the younger and more hot-blooded clergy and to revive the chastened passion of the Republicans; its ultimate effects were far-reaching, for it destroyed the hopes of amicable settlement which at that time had begun to take visible shape.

* Letter to Tipperary Board of Guardians, June, 1916.

The rebellion had shocked the more sober elements of society. It had brought them face to face with the realities of Civil War. The gaunt ruins of Sackville Street were so many signposts pointing towards conciliation. The Government seized the opportunity to reopen the negotiations which had failed on the eve of the war. Mr Asquith himself crossed over to Dublin and went out of his way – some thought too far out of his way – to be conciliatory to the rebels. Mr Lloyd George – who has since shown his abilities as a negotiator on a larger field – was charged with the task of bringing parties together. He was within an ace of success.

The Ulster Unionist Council met. Under the terms of the Ulster Covenant the Unionists of all the nine Ulster counties had bound themselves to stand or fall together. But if the proposals of the Government were to be accepted, it was necessary that the counties of Cavan, Monaghan, and Donegal should stand out and accept the rule of the Parliament in Dublin. After long consideration they agreed to waive their rights under the Covenant and to place themeselves at the disposal of the Council. It has been said that they only yielded to the argument that thus they would 'kill Home Rule'. But that is not true. The effect of their decision on the fate of the Home Rule Bill was never even mentioned. The only question discussed was that of national expediency, the desirability of bringing Ireland into line on the side of the Allies, then hard pressed, and of presenting a united front to the world. And indeed, had the decision of the Ulster Council been taken as a matter of party tactics, it would have been an extremely venturesome gamble. For the Convention of the Nationalists of Ulster, which followed later, agreed to the exclusion of the six counties of Antrim, Down, Armagh, Londonderry, Tyrone, and Fermanagh from the operation of the Home Rule Act. There was, however, one point on which the parties were not agreed. The Unionists wished the exclusion of the six counties to be 'definite,' while the Nationalists declared that is should be 'provisional,' *i.e.* that, as Mr Lloyd George had proposed, it should be subject to revision, as part of a scheme of general Imperial reconstruction, a year after the termination of the war.

The difference was serious, indeed it was fundamental, but it might perhaps have been adjusted in view of the great Imperial necessities of the time, the shock of Civil War, and the desire of the Unionists and of Mr Redmond that Ireland should play her full part in the great world struggle.

Thus, as Mr Redmond saw clearly, did Ireland out of evil get a second and most unexpected opportunity. Once, in 1914, had the chance presented itself, and she let it slip. And now it came to her two years later. Had Ireland taken the first chance, and said to Britain, 'Your cause is mine,' there is no reasonable measure of self-government, short of separation. which she might not have asked for and received. Irish Unionists, even though they might have but languid confidence in the merits of Irish administration, would have felt it churlish to deny men who had taken their share of the war; they would have thought that, after all, they had been true to the flag, and would have been content to bury the old animosities and suspicious in the trenches where the wearers of the Orange and the Green lay entombed together.

After the rebellion Ireland could not hope for such full concessions, though even then she might have got much, but, in the spirit of Dr O'Dwyer's letter, she again flung away the substance for the shadow. The Roman Catholic Hierarchy of Ulster had been the bitterest opponents of exclusion in the Nationalist Convention; their colleague in the south set the heather on fire. At once Sinn Fein raised a cry against Partition. The pause in the negotiations, caused by the different limitations set on exclusion by the Unionists and Nationalists, gave the chorus time to gain volume, and as it gained in volume so did Mr Redmond find himself compelled to stiffen his back on the point of 'provisional' exclusion, or to see his power, already waning, disappear altogether. On the Unionists the effect of Dr O'Dwyer's letter and the outburst of Republican fury was to convince them that concessions made to promote unity would be made in vain, while the Government saw in the unrepentant attitude of Sinn Fein a confirmation of the view of the southern Unionists that the establishment of a Parliament in which Sinn Fein would be powerful, and while Ireland was in such an unsettled condition, would be a dangerous experiment, which might materially prejudice the conduct of the war. Accordingly on July 24th – by a strange coincidence it was on that same day two years before that the conference at Buckingham Palace had broken down – Mr Asquith announced in Parliament that the Government had abandoned the attempt at a settlement.

The history of these few weeks has been thus dwelt upon as one of the most pregnant phases of the revolutionary movement. It reveals Sinn Fein as the sworn enemy of any attempt at settlement by consent, a fact of the highest importance in the consideration of contemporary Irish politics. From a broader point of view it is deeply interesting in that it is perhaps the first instance of the Roman Catholic Hierarchy ranging itself on the side of revolution based upon the most extreme doctrines of Socialism.

As has been said, the southern Unionists had, while the negotiations were in progress, impressed on the Government the risk of erecting an Irish Legislature in the then state of the country. It has been the fashion to treat warnings from that quarter as the creations of a fevered and prejudiced imagination, but in this instance at least they had solid foundation. Even while they were being uttered Count Bernstorff was informing his Foreign Office that the reorganisation of the Irish Republicans was proceeding apace, and that he had supplied them with the money of which they stood in need. The Republican junta in America observed the action of the Bishop of Limerick with great approval, and took measures to provide him with a colleague of pronounced views. It chanced that about that time the bishopric of Cork fell vacant. Among the prominent candidates was one of moderate opinions and friendly to the British connection. Another was Dr Daniel Cohalan. Count Bernstorff greatly interested himself in the matter, and on August 23rd telegraphed as follows to the German Foreign Office:

'The Bishop of Cork having died, there is a sharp contest over the succession. The present Assistant Bishop, Daniel Cohalan, is the choice of the local clergy; but England is using unusual efforts to have – appointed. – is strongly anti-German, although Germany, at our request, released him shortly after the outbreak of war. Assistant-Bishop Cohalan is cousin of Judge Cohalan, and strongly Nationalist and pro-German. He was the intermediary between the insurgent Cork Volunteers and the British military authorities, and publicly exposed the gross breach of faith of the English with the surrendered men.

Hence the effort to defeat him through the English Envoy at the Vatican. . . . It would have a great moral effect in Rome if Cohalan were chosen. If Germany can exert any influence to bring about this result it would defeat the English intrigue aimed against her interests.'

What efforts Germany made must be a matter of surmise. Certain it is that Dr Danial Cohalan is now the Bishop of Cork, an earnest labourer in the political vineyard.

CHAPTER XII

MAKERS OF MISCHIEF

For a moment let us turn our eyes from the United Kingdom to the Continent, that we may view Irish affairs in their relation to the war. While Sinn Fein was making it final preparations for rebellion – the coincidence could hardly have been accidental – France was battling for her very life; while Dublin was being battered out of shape Verdun was crumbling out of existence. The battle of Jutland was fought in May, and was celebrated by the Irish Republicans in verses recited, amid wild applause, in the revolutionary concert halls.* While the Government at home was striving for settlement, and Sinn Fein was making it impossible, the battles of the Somme were raging. While Dr O'Dwyer was denouncing the brutality of General Maxwell, Nurse Cavell and Captain Fryatt were being done to death by the allies of the Irish Separatists. As always, England's extremity was Ireland's opportunity, and the Republicans used it to the full.

Their attitude was both singular and significant. It might have been expected that the failure of the rising would have left them in a chastened mood, of which their moderate leaders would have taken advantage to recall them from the dangerous

* A couple of verses will show the nature of this effusion:

The Rats Came Out.

Britannia rules the waves, Britons never shall be slaves!
  We've been told the tale so often that we've scarcely room for doubt;
Irish rebels in their graves, done to death by cowardly knaves
  Would sleep peacefully, I'm certain, if they knew the rats came out....

The blood of murdered Irishmen appeals to Heaven once again
  The fleet that shelled old Dublin town have got a clean knockout.
True Irish hearts will ever pray that God will speed the coming day
  When Britain's fleet is swept away when next the rats come out.

paths into which they had strayed. Conciliation was in the air. Mr Asquith had been polite to the point of flattery in his talks with the captive rebels, the spirit of negotiation was abroad, and they not only stood aloof, but bestirred themselves to prevent agreement. Some little sign from them would have done much to diminish the rigour of Mr Redmond's attitude, but it was not given. Whether he desired it on no, he was forced, if he and his party were not to be swept from the stage, to meet the Ulster demand with an uncompromising negative.

Nay, more. Sinn Fein took heart from the negotiations set on foot by Mr Lloyd George. Outwardly denouncing the Government as barbarously tyrannical, it secretly construed its desire for settlement as a proof of abject weakness and grew more insolent and defiant the while it pursued its negotiations with Germany. Sinn Fein Clubs sprang up all over the country in hundreds; the Irish Volunteers swelled from a brigade into a couple of Army Corps.

Numerous attempts were made by the more moderate Nationalists to stem the Republican advance by diverting the popular demand into less dangerous channels. The Irish Nation League was formed at Omagh in August, as a half-way house between the Parliamentarians and the Republicans. It came to nothing. Mr Redmond tried to retain the constituencies by motions in Parliament for inquiries into the events of the rebellion, the abolition of martial law, and the release of the deportees. The Government made some concessions. Sir John Maxwell was recalled; a new Chief Secretary was appointed; over three-quarters of the interned prisoners were released. It was all in vain: Sinn Fein pursued its course unmoved and unrelenting. Throughout the autumn it was beseeching Germany to send an expedition, and to establish bases for submarines and Zeppelins in the west of Ireland. In December it was pressing the German Government for a favourable reply, at the very moment that the *Manchester Guardian* was calling for a general amnesty as a step to perfect harmony, and that the *Daily News* was proclaiming that it was useless to expect any improvement in Ireland's sentiments while the rebels were interned at Frongoch. Six hundred were released, and Sinn Fein became more irreconcilable.

In February Count Plunkett was elected member for North

Roscommon with over three thousand votes against less than seven hundred cast for Mr Redmond's candidate. And then Mr Redmond made a last attempt to stem the current, with a motion proposed by Mr T. P. O'Connor:

'That, with a view to strengthening the hands of the Allies in achieving the recognition of the equal rights of small nations and the principle of nationality against the opposition German principles of military domination and Government without the consent of the governed, it is essential without further delay to confer upon Ireland the free institutions long promised to her.'*

Mr Lloyd George, who by this time was Prime Minister, speaking as a Home Ruler, said that the Cabinet was ready to give self-government to that part of Ireland which desired it, but not to that part which rejected it. It was impossible to force any one part of Ireland to live under a law which it did not approve, least of all in the circumstances then existing. There could be no question of imposing 'Home Rule' on the people of the north-east, as hostile to Irish rule as the rest of Ireland is to British rule, yea, and as ready to rebel against this as the rest of Ireland is to revolt against British rule. He then moved the following amendment:

'That this House would welcome a settlement which would produce a better understanding between Ireland and the rest of the United Kingdom, but considers it impossible to impose by force on any section or part of Ireland a form of Government which has not their assent.'

Mr Redmond rejected the amendment. The time for conferences and negotiations, he said, had gone by. He denied the right of minorities to call check to the spirit of a nation; he demanded the Home Rule Act, the whole Act, and nothing but the Act. The state of Ireland, he said, was very serious. The constitutional movement had, by forty years of toil, practically eliminated the revolutionary agitation, and now its work was being wrecked in sight of port.

Were one disposed for controversy, it might be pointed out that Mr Redmond put the effect of the constitutional upon the revolutionary movement too high, and placed too generous

* March 7th, 1917.

an estimate on the value of the Home Rule Act as an implement of conciliation. For at the very time when the success of the measure was secured, and even before it was introduced, the forces of revolution, which Mr Redmond declared had been practically eliminated, were deciding the measure and concerting rebellion. But that may pass.

Having made his protest, Mr Redmond left the House with his followers, and the debate ended without a decision being taken. The next day the Nationalists published a manifesto, proclaiming their loyalty to the cause of the Allies, though compelled to go into opposition to the Government, and appealing to the Irishmen of America and the Dominions to put pressure on the British Government to act towards Ireland in conformity with the principles for which the Allies were fighting in Europe.

Even this dramatic and adroit move met with no response from Sinn Fein. Then, if ever, was its opportunity. The wording of Mr Redmond's manifesto could be read to include a demand for self-government on the broadest lines. 'The principles for which the Allies are fighting' might even be construed to mean complete independence. Why then did Sinn Fein remain unmoved? Surely, for one reason only – that it knew that Mr Redmond, though he would have taken the widest form of self-government if it were offered him, did not contemplate severance from the Empire. Because of that he was still the West Briton, the helot and the traitor.

An opportunity soon occurred for Sinn Fein to show its opinion of Mr Redmond and to give an answer to the Prime Minister's suggestion for settlement. Major Willie Redmond was killed at Messines, dying, by a pathetic coincidence, among the Ulstermen. Mr De Valera was nominated for East Clare, Major Redmond's constituency. On the next day, June 15th, 1917, the Government proclaimed a general amnesty and all the Irish prisoners were released. They availed themselves of their liberty to make speeches of the most seditious character up and down the island, declaring that 'England is beaten to the ropes;' 'France is bled white;' 'Germany is no enemy of Ireland.' 'England,' cried one orator, 'has been an enemy in the past, why should we not assist her enemies now?' Another speaker supplied the answer: 'Get ready; keep getting ready;

when the call comes stand to arms.[9]

By this time America was in the war. But that did not prevent 'The Provisional Government of the Irish Republic' from sending its 'Ambassador,' Dr Patrick McCartan,* to President Wilson and Congress, with a communication which contained the following passage:

'Our Nationalism is not founded upon grievances. We are opposed not to English misgovernment but to English government in Ireland. . . . While prepared, when the opportunity arises, to assert our independence by the one force which commands universal respect and to accept aid from any quarter to that end, we hope Americans will see their way to aid in doing for Ireland what they did for Cuba.'

Considering the circumstances, it is probable that no more astonishing communication was ever made to the head of a great nation than this. It was presented in the name of the Irish Republic, an organisation hostile and rebellious to a State on whose side America was then fighting and in active alliance with Germany, with whom America was at war. It was framed by a junta one of whose leading members had been specially recommended as a reliable agent for organising sabotage in the United States. And America was asked to put pressure on England to give Ireland that right of secession which half a century before she had refused to her own disentient States at the cost of four years of bitter war.

It is probable that in sending this message, and in the choice of the ambassador who should convey it, Sinn Fein was inspired as much by a desire to insult the President as by any hope of receiving a favourable reply. In the days when America was still neutral the Irish-Americans had abused the head of the State with a freedom which on this side of the Atlantic it is difficult to understand. The exchange of neutrality for active co-operation with the Allies drove them to frenzy. It paralysed their energies, it deprived them of the services of Count Bern-

* Dr McCartan was at that time a fugitive from Ireland. He is now Dispensary Doctor for the Omagh District Council and has leave of absence, his return to his duties being delayed for what have been stated in the Council to be 'well-known reasons.' He is also a Sinn Fein M.P., and is, or recently was, an inmate of an American gaol.

storff, Von Igel, and the rest of the Teutonic horde; they saw their fellow Irishmen in America swept into the maëlstrom of the conscription which they had successfully resisted in Ireland as the barbarous implement of bloodthirsty tyranny. In their distress these hyphenated citizens of the United States, notwithstanding that myriads of Irishmen were fighting for America, still continued to plot for Germany's success, though force of circumstances compelled them to transfer their main energies from New York to Berlin.

In America what work was done was through the Society of the Friends of Irish Freedom, founded in 1916, of which Mr Jeremiah O'Leary was President, with Professor Kuno Meyer and Mr St John Gaffney, ex-Consul-General of the United States at Munich, as his principle colleagues. When America entered the war Kuno Meyer returned to Germany, where he again worked with St John Gaffney and a Mr Chatterton-Hill, and founded the German-Irish Society, which was the European counterpart of the Friends of Irish Freedom. Among the officials of this Society were Herr Erzberger, Baron von Reichthofen, Count Westarp, the leader of the Junkers in the Reichstag, Professor Edouard Meyer, Professor Schiemann, and many other eminent persons. The Society ran a monthy review, *Irische Blätter*, of which Chatterton-Hill was editor.

It is important to observe that the first number of this magazine is appeared in May, 1917, a month after the United States had declared war against Germany, driven to that extreme measure, so repugnant to the genius of the American people, by the conviction that German success would be fatal to civilisation, liberty, and moral law. Yet in the opening address of the German-Irish Society and in the pages of *Irische Blätter* we find the following passages:

'The war has proved that Germany has very few friends. But the Irish have acted as friends at home as well as in the United States, and Germany must not underestimate the value of Irish friendship. From the beginning of the war the American-Irish adopted the German cause with enthusiasm, and in alliance with the German-Americans conducted a courageous fight for true neutrality. There is no doubt that, but for the support of the Irish organisations, the politically unorganised German-Americans would have been condemned to impotence. . . . The

German-Irish Society will devote its energies to reopening Ireland to the world, and *especially* to *Germany*. It will . . . generally and in every way further the progressive development of the Emerald Isle in the interests of the German as well as the Irish people.'

So much for the inaugural address. Two points may be noted. First, the Irish activities which so embarrassed the American Government in the period of neutrality. Second, the promise to throw Ireland open especially to Germany, whose crimes had dragged America reluctantly into war. The following are passages from page 102 of *Irische Blätter* of May, 1917:

'When the West-Irish harbours serve as bases for U-boats, and a large part of the country is in the hands of one of the organised revolutionary armies, then will England's rule over the sea quickly come to an end. Not only can many English ships carrying munitions and the necessaries of life be sunk, but others can be captured and towed into Irish ports to supply the Irish army with munitions and the Irish people with food. Thus would England be handed over to her enemies and the war quickly brought to an end.'

Here we pause to contemplate the prospect opened up, not only for Great Britain but for America, by the Friends of Irish Freedom and the German-Irish Society. Secured in their possession of the Irish coast, the U-boats will have the Atlantic traffic at their mercy. American transports can be 'sunk without trace,' their ships, like those carrying the Red Ensign, can be sunk or captured at will. The war would be swiftly brought to an end, and America would share in the defeat. And this was the programme of American citizens, including a Judge and an ex-Consul-General, directed not, as in the case of England, against a nation which had imposed her rule upon them, but against the country of their own choosing.

Meanwhile in Ireland Sinn Fein was prospering amazingly. De Valera was elected for East Clare by a huge majority; Mr Cosgrave won the suffrages of Kilkenny; in South Longford Mr MacGuinness wrested a seat from the Parliamentarians. A solemn resolution was taken that no representatives of Sinn Fein would recognise British rule by taking their seats at Westminster, thus incidentally sparing themselves the painful necessity of committing wilful and deliberate perjury. The Clubs continued to multiply,* and the armies, to which *Irische Blätter* so hopefully referred, to increase.† The negotiations which had been in progress in December had for the time come to an end in consequence of Germany's refusal to send troops – she was by now beginning to feel the pinch – though she was ready and willing to send arms and provide money.

Disappointed in their hope of another Civil War, the high spirit of the Sinn Feiners found an outlet in those forms of crime which habitually distinguish moments of political excitement in Ireland – shooting of police, robbery of arms, cattle-driving, and boycotting. One case of boycotting deserves commemoration. In November, 1917, Mrs Ryan, a schoolmistress, was driven out of her school by a body of Sinn Fein and pickets were posted to prevent it being reopened until another teacher was appointed. Mrs Ryan's offence was that, on the occasion of Lord Kitchener's death in 1916, she had played the 'Dead March' in *Saul* in the presence of her pupils. What is one to think of a great national movement for liberty that can descend to such pettiness?

Again, it is significant that these activities coincided with an attempt to reach a settlement of the Irish question more elaborate and containing greater presages of success than ever before. Out of twelve months of groping for a possible solution emerged the Convention, to which were nominated, or in some cases elected, 103 members, representative of every shade of opinion, and perhaps more representative of Ireland as a whole than any other body which had assembled since the Union. Great hopes were attached to the meeting of this assembly, and therefore it at once became the object of Sinn Fein to wreck them.

From the outset Sinn Fein stood aloof, refusing to send delegates to the Convention. It departed from its attitude of neutrality when it began to get abroad that a most promising spirit of harmony and goodwill pervaded the meetings. To

* At the Sinn Fein Convention, October 25th, 1917, 1009 Clubs were represented by 1700 delegates. It was stated by the Secretary that the total number of Clubs was about 1200, with a membership of about 250,000.

† Mr Duke, Chief Secretary for Ireland, estimated that the Sinn Fein Volunteers numbered 200,000 men in October, 1917. – *Hansard*, October 24th, 1917.

prevent any such alarming development Sinn Fein became threatening and disorderly, to such a point that Mr Lloyd George had to give a solemn warning in Parliament that he would not allow incitements to rebellion, nor preparation for rebellion, nor any separatists propaganda for the 'sovereign independence' of Ireland.

Then the Roman Catholic Church took fright. The Bishops of Kildare, Clonfert, and Achonry preached in condemnation of the revolutionary doctrines. A letter from Cardinal Logue was read in all the churches of the Archdiocese of Armagh on November 25th, in which he condemned:

'an utopian and ill-conceived agitation, which could not fail to be followed by present suffering, disorder, and danger, and which in the future would surely produce disaster, defeat, and ruin – and all this in pursuit of a dream which no man of sound sense could hope to see realised: the establishment of an Irish Republic whether by an appeal to the potentates of Europe sitting in the Peace Conference or by an appeal to force.'

Thus did the elders of the Church throw over the younger clergy and others, more mature in age, but equally hot in blood, and say to Sinn Fein 'Thus far and no further'.

Sinn Fein was as deaf to the orders of the Church as it had been to British advances and Nationalist desire for settlement. *New Ireland* replied to the Bishop that 'Ireland had learned in a terrible school not to regard eminent ecclesiastics as the supreme authority in question of politics'. Mr De Valera, protesting his attachment to religion, maintained that the laws of the Church did not condemn his doctrines.

So closed the year 1917, Unionists and Nationalists striving hard and honestly to find a basis for agreement; Sinn Fein striving hard and lawlessly to make their efforts of no effect. In order to acheive its purpose Sinn Fein at this time made a further movement towards the party of revolutionary Labour. *New Ireland,* in October, enunciated the opinion that of all European parties Socialism most nearly approached the idealism of Christianity, an assertion not in itself remarkable, but interesting as marking the development of the alliance which had begun before the rebellion. This further advance towards the extreme Labour Party was perhaps in some measure Sinn

Fein's reply to the admonitions of the Church. We have seen how in its early days the movement suffered no little damage from the suggestion that it had anti-clerical implications, and it is possible that it now turned towards a party which had scant reverence for ecclesiastical thunderings to make up for any losses it might sustain among its more devout adherents.

But there was another reason as well. The negotiations between Sinn Fein and Germany which had broken down in the closing days of 1916, had been resumed, and this time with more practical result. True, Germany was unable to send men, for these were becoming more scarce every day, but she could send arms and was making elaborate preparations to send them.

St Patrick's Day, 1918, was celebrated in Berlin with great enthusiasm, in spite of the fact that, except for Dr Chatterton-Hill, the celebrants were entirely German. Count Westarp presided at a banquet at the Hotel Adlon, when speeches were delivered quite in the vein of those of the Watertoast Sympathisers. Their tone can be the better appreciated if it be remembered that, when they were spoken, Germany was preparing for her last desperate throw and sorely needed every atom of help that she could get.

Count Westarp laid down the doctrine that 'a people which was incapable of a righteous hatred towards their mortal enemies was also incapable of any profound devotion to their own cause'. England, he went on, which had been Ireland's mortal enemy, was now Germany's mortal enemy as well. Germany had never thought before the war that it would be her mission to destroy England's maritime supremacy – here one pauses to reflect on the articles concocted by Casement and Kuno Meyer in 1911, and the toast of '*Der Tag*' – but she had been forced into the task and was in a position to accomplish it, thanks to her numerical superiority and to the U-boats. Councillor of Legation Von Strumm, who represented the Foreign Office, played his best card to his partner's lead. It was recently reported, he said, that Ireland was quiet and that an Irish Convention has assembled which was to settle her destinies to the general satisfaction. But now talk of the Convention had ceased, and Lord French had gone to Dublin to 'tranquillise' Ireland. They knew what that tranquillising meant:

the people of Ceylon and the Transvaal could tell them. If, as Mr Asquith had said, England's territorial conquests in the war were to come before the Peace Conference, Ireland should come before it too. Lord French might conquer Ireland, but he would never subjugate her, and Ireland could always count on the sympathy of the German people.

Dr Chatterton-Hill, in his response to these assurances, described Sinn Fein as 'that great political, economic, and cultural movement which recognised England as the evil genius of Ireland, and which thwarted her and combated her in every direction'. And then he announced that 'Ireland was on the eve of great events'. For his audience this dark utterance held no mystery. To aid her great offensive on the Western Front, Germany had arranged to land a big supply of arms and ammunition in Ireland. Less than a month after Dr Chatterton-Hill's prophecy, an emissary landed on the coast of Clare to announce its imminent fulfilment. He was an Irishman, one Dowling, *alias* O'Brien, one of the few who had yielded to Casement's seductions at Limburg. A few weeks later, in May, U-boats left Cuxhaven laden with arms and ammunition, but never reached their destination. And then came the 18th of July, when Ludendorff played his last throw at the Marne and lost.

So perished Casement's dreams of German dominion and the hopes cherished by Sinn Fein of a German invasion of Ireland.

But Sinn Fein had gained something by its activities. In March Mr Redmond died, broken-hearted by the failure of his policy and by domestic sacrifices made in vain, and with him disappeared the most formidable opponent of Republicanism in the Nationalist ranks. The Convention, too, had failed to arrive at a settlement. Sir Horace Plunkett summed up the cause of its failure in two words: 'Ulster and Customs.'

More or less directly, Sinn Fein had been instrumental in developing these obstacles. It had stiffened the Nationalist demands and the Unionist resistance. It had widened the gulf between the two great schools of Irish thought until it became unbridgeable. There was room for accommodation, though cramped and un-comfortable, in previous measures of Home Rule – the exclusion of Unionist Ulster, for example. But that device, artificial and difficult at the best, became absolutely imposible in a scheme which gave the Irish Government the power of erecting a tariff wall. The success of Sinn Fein in upsetting the attempts at settlement by consent so often repeated swept away all the ambiguities which had theretofore obscured the Irish question, and made it a clear issue.

These successes, however, were only partial and negative. They were more than counterbalanced by the defeat of Germany. Deprived of her assistance, Sinn Fein had to seek other alliances, and in the article in *New Ireland* we have an indication of the direction in which its thoughts were turning.

CHAPTER XIII

THE BOLSHEVIK ALLIANCE

TIME was when the American-Irish were united with the Russian sojourners in the great Republic in very cordial friendship. Those were the days when Bokhara and Merv were on men's lips, when maps of Central Asia were in demand, when people shuddered at the name of Penjdeh, and the slumbers of British statesmen were troubled by visions of the Colossus with one foot planted at Archangel and the other at Cape Comorin. The Irish in America also had their visions, but they were dissipated by the war of 1906 and the destruction of Rodjestvensky's Armada. They transferred their hopes to Germany, only to see them in their turn shattered at the Marne. But in her death agony Germany had constructed a force to which the Irish revolutionaries turned in their distress, a Russia, no longer the especial enemy of England, but the enemy of every nation that aspired to be civilised.

The way to this renewal of the old friendship had been smoothed by Connolly during his sojourn in America. His hereditary Fenianism, his ardent assertion of nationality and his contempt of the policy of Mr Redmond and the Parliamentarians, gave him easy access to such men as John Devoy and Jeremiah O'Leary, while his career as an organiser of the Industrial Workers of the World brought him in contact with the potential Bolsheviki. Accordingly we find the merits of Lenin's Government extolled increasingly as the fortunes of Germany wavered in the balance and declined. Among a certain section of the Irish Republicans there would appear to have been at first a certain hesitancy, begotten perhaps of the growing fear that the creation of the Soviet Government had reacted injuriously to Germany, perhaps – for there is a party of the Right as well as of the Left in Sinn Fein – of an instinctive dislike of the new doctrines.

But there were voices crying in the wilderness. As has been

shown, Connolly's robust nationalism and the practicality of his methods had drawn towards him men like Pearse, who gradually became imbued with his economic doctrines and carried the infection into the Sinn Fein organisation. There were others whose sole object was to attain independence, and who were not too nice or curious as to the source from which they got assistance, and others again who were revolutionaries first, last, and all the time, and whose aim was destruction. In a movement such as is Sinn Fein, whose ultimate sanction is force, such elements are certain to overbear the intellectuals and idealists, even if they have no direct encouragement from its leaders.

In this instance the extreme revolutionary section and the Bolshevik alliance had firm friends in the inner circle of Sinn Fein. The men who, in America, played the leading part in the formation of the new alliance were Dr Patrick McCartan and Liam (*anglicè* William) Mellowes. A few words are here necessary to explain the position held by these men in the Sinn Fein organisation and the nature of their work in America.

When the United States went into the war and Count Bernstorff left Washington, the methods of the transatlantic conspirators had to be completely changed, and Mellowes and McCartan were charged with the direction of affairs. Both had left Ireland after the rebellion, in which Mellowes commanded a force operating in County Galway. There is reason to believe that he had spent some time in Germany after his escape from Ireland, and it is certain that in New York he was in association with a Baron von Rechlinghausen, a German agent, one of their objects being to forward money to the Turks and to establish a mysterious Turkish organisation in America. The other, and the main object, of this trio – Mellowes, McCartan, and Rechlinghausen – was to organise another revolution in Ireland in the spring of 1918. In the preceding chapter we have seen how this plot failed, how Dowling was captured on landing in County Clare, and the arms shipped at Cuxhaven failed to reach their destination.

The main cause of the failure was the arrest of McCartan and Mellowes in October 1917. The 'ambassador' was arrested at Halifax while on his way to Ireland, while at the same time Mellowes was captured in New York on the eve of his departure, to use his own words, 'for the Easter sports of 1918.'

Documents were found in Mellowes' possession dealing with the secret history of the 1916 rebellion, which could not have reached any one who was not entirely in the confidence of Sinn Fein. One of them clears up the mystery, which puzzled the Rebellion Commission, of the famous order for the precautionary arrest of the revolutionary leaders which was read by Alderman Kelly at a meeting of the Dublin Corporation on April 19th, 1916, four days before the rising. The order was given to Alderman Kelly by Mr Little, the editor of *New Ireland*, as having been issued from Dublin Castle. The document found in Mellowes' possession, however, shows that it was a forgery, done by the Sinn Fein extremists to force the wavering hands of Professor MacNeill and to precipitate the rebellion.* In both these purposes it succeeded: MacNeill gave the orders for the Easter Monday operations, though, as we have seen he cancelled them.

So seriously did the arrest of Mellowes and McCartan compromise the revolutionary plans, that in November Sinn Fein was compelled to send a long despatch to their New York agents with a new set of instructions. This despatch was carried by a certain Thomas Welsh, who was arrested as he was disembarking from the *Celtic* and was taken from him as he was attempting to tear it to pieces.†

'General' Mellowes, therefore, holds a high place in Sinn Fein, but that held by Dr Cartan is still higher. He is a medical man, a Fellow of the College of Surgeons, and the Sinn Fein 'ambassador' to the United States, in which capacity we have already seen him approaching the head of the State. And in that capacity also he was negotiating with the 'ambassador' of the Russian Soviet Republic. Of the nature of Mellows' connection with the Bolshevists we have no precise knowledge except that imparted by the Irish Labour organ, the *Voice of Labour*, in the following paragraph:

'Almost every message we got from America tells us how strongly an old friend, Liam Mellowes, stands up for the Russian fighters for freedom.‡

Dr McCartan's relations are infinitely more definite. So far

* *Freeman's Journal*, November 29th, 1917.

† *Ibid.*, November 27th, 1917.

‡ *Voice of Labour*, June 21st, 1919.

back as January, 1918, his sympathy with the Russian Soviet Government was recorded by *New Ireland*, a Sinn Fein paper, and urged as a reason for his selection as candidate for South Armagh:

'Dr McCartan is imprisoned in America for his activities as a worker in the cause of Irish Republicanism. He went to America as an accredited representative of the movement. We know that his views are very strong upon the importance of using the Russian democratic programme for the benefit of Ireland, and of allying ourselves with Russian democrats, and with real democrats throughout the world.'*

During the following year the world shuddered at the infamies of Lenin and Trotsky and their Commissaries, but the Bolshevik enthusiasm of the Sinn Fein ambassador suffered no abatement. The Soviet Government sent an ambassador to America, a Mr L. Martens, who was rapturously greeted by the Irish revolutionaries. In the spring of 1919 an exchange of notes took place between him and the Irish envoy. The circumstances which led to it are not without interest. A story was going the round of the American and British Press that the Soviet Republic was subsidising Sinn Fein to the tune of some millions of roubles. The moderate Sinn Feiners contradicted the assertion and took occasion to express disaproval of the Soviet methods. This would seem to have given pain to Mr Martens, for he straightway addressed a letter to Dr McCartan, asking whether these sentiments were shared by his government, and incidentally denying that the Russian Republic had sent any funds to Sinn Fein.

In his reply Dr McCartan disclaimed the authorship of the report about the subsidies, and with regard to the more important query said:

'The 4,000,000 people of the Republic of Ireland, in their struggle to free themselves from military subjugation by an Empire of 400,000,000, want and welcome the aid of all free men, of all free peoples, and, certainly, of the free men of the Russian Socialist Federated Soviet Republic.'

He then proceeds to say that the Irish people do not believe the account of Soviet rule retailed by the Northcliffe Press, nor the stories of Soviet outrages told by the British Government,

* *New Ireland*, January 26th, 1918.

which was itself participating in the butcheries of Koltchak, Denikin, and Mannerheim, and then he thus concludes:

'Hence, between the gallant, starving, isolated Russians striving against alien enemies to found securely in Russia a government of the people, by the people, for the people, and the Irish also isolated in their struggle against British armies of occupation to found securely the Republic of Ireland, there can exist only that sense of brotherhood which a common experience endured for a common purpose can alone induce.'*

These assurances would appear to have been entirely satisfactory to Lenin, for in June Tchitcherin, the Bolshevik Foreign Minister, sent a radio message to Bela Kun, which was published by *L'Humanité* on June 16th. The message ran thus:

'Whereas in nearly every country our compatriots have neither protection nor representation, we have put all foreigners in the same position, and we will afford them no special protection. Exception will be made, however, in the case of the Irish and the Egyptians, and of any other nationality oppressed by the Allies.'

Mr Cathal O'Shannon remarks that 'for this special mark of honour both Irish and Egyptians will be grateful to the Soviet Republic'.†

We shall doubtless be assured, as we were assured in respect of Germany, that there is no alliance between the Soviet Republic and the Republicans of Ireland. Perhaps not – why bandy phrases? – but there is a very substantial understanding. It is abundantly clear that the intellectual and idealistic side of the revolutionary movement had surrendered to the proletarian. There are, of course, some who view this development with distrust and dislike, among them Mr Hegarty, but as a whole Sinn Fein has obeyed the ordinary law of revolutionary evolution and no longer controls the force which it set in motion.

It will be convenient at this point to consider the particular causes which impel Sinn Fein willy-nilly to gravitate towards the left, over and above the ordinary revolutionary tendency just alluded to. There is first the belief that Russian Communism

* *New York Call*, May 10th, 1919, reprinted in the *Voice of Labour*, June 21st. The same issue of the latter paper testifies to the sturdy championship of the Bolshevists by Liam Mellowes.

† *Voice of Labour*, July 5th, 1919.

is destined to triumph, as set forth in a Sinn Fein paper:

'Their ideas are in the ascendant and against them mere military force is powerless. They have affected Germany deeply, they will certainly affect France, Italy will follow easily enough, England is doubtful, and the United States will remain quite impervious. America will have only American democracy, which is merely snobbery and conceit under another name.'*

Holding this faith, Sinn Fein sees in the spread of Bolshevism through Europe an embarrassment for Great Britain more serious even than the threats of German militarism, and all the more serious because of the possibility that it may invade Great Britain, as no Continental Power could ever do. Sinn Fein has accordingly been impelled to enter into relations with John Maclean, the Bolshevik Consul-General in Glasgow, and the Clyde Committee. Messages passed between them just before the General Election, giving reciprocal assurances of co-operation and asseverating the harmony of their respective aims.

Next, Sinn Fein has to consider its own position in Ireland. It now holds seventy-three seats, but it must have doubts whether it will hold as many at the next General Election. Some of them it owes to the self-abnegation of the Labour Party, which will hardly be so self-denying on the next occasion. And Labour has been growing in strength. The affiliated membership of the Irish Trade Union and Labour Party Congress in 1912 was 70,000; in 1916 it had risen to 120,000; in 1918 250 delegates claimed to represent 250,000 members, while between 1916 and 1918 the income had increased from £410 to £1,610. Labour is therefore a thing to be reckoned with, not only for its voting strength but as a field for recruiting.

And there is this further consideration which can hardly be absent from the calculations of De Valera. In all countries the rural population is the last to catch the fever of revolution. In Ireland the change from tenancy to ownership is bound to operate as an additional prophylactic against infection. Three hundred thousand agricultural proprietors have been created, one hundred thousand more have entered into arrangements to purchase, and all of them on easy terms which enable them to resell their properties at a large profit. These men are not inflammable material, nor are the dealings of the Soviet Repub-

* *New Ireland*, January 12th, 1918.

lic with the peasantry of Russia likely to arouse their enthusiasm – when they get to know them. Sinn Fein is therefore thrown back perforce on the urban population, where revolutionary Labour is in the ascendant. Such a combination of forces compels Sinn Fein to accept the alliance, much as some of its members may mistrust it, of the Bolshevik element in the revolutionary movement.

Were the revolutionaries to achieve their object, it is probable that the new Irish Republic would be the theatre of a sanguinary struggle between the constructive and destructive wings of the movement. But until that moment Sinn Fein ignores the probable catastrophe of the future in order to win the possible triumph of the present. Indeed, it is compelled to ignore it. It is being driven headlong by furies of its own creation into paths which, most likely, it never contemplated ten, or even five years ago. It has proclaimed a Republic, elected a President, nominated its envoys, established its Parliament. To descend from such altitudes to an acceptance of local self-government would be suicide. It would perish under the ridicule of the world and the execrations of the people it has deceived. Not one man of its leaders would ever again have a place in the public life of Ireland, for Great Britain could never trust the word of men who formed alliances with Germany and avowed their desire to destroy her in the hour of her sorest need.

Sinn Fein, therefore, must go forward because it cannot go back. But it cannot go forward alone, it must have an ally. Where is one to be found? France, to whom revolutionary Ireland was wont to look, turns her back on her today. America may express a platonic desire to see the Irish question settled, and even settled on broad lines, but Sinn Fein knows in its heart that neither America, nor any other Power in friendship with Great Britain, would formulate or support a demand that she should concede independence to Ireland, when the very men who demand it have proclaimed that the loss of Ireland means the loss of her place in the world. So fully does Sinn Fein realise that fact that already they are exchanging the language of appeal and flattery for the language of menace to the United States.

To what, then, can Sinn Fein turn for assistance other than the revolutionary movement which knows neither boundaries, nor international obligations, nor scruples, and which itself is using every device, however disgraceful, to gain adherents wherever it can find them? Were the position thus nakedly presented to some leaders of Sinn Fein, they would repudiate it, though there are many that would not – Mr Walsh, for instance, the member for Cork City, who said at Blackpool that 'if the devil himself and all the devils in hell were up against the British Government the Irish people would be pro-devil and pro-hell'.* But they comfortably blind themselves to it when they enter into relations with the extreme Labour Party.

Mr de Blacam states the case very clearly in the following passage:

'In the great national boycott of the English language, English manufacturers, English institutions, Labour will play a large – perhaps the largest – part. Labour has practical work before it no less than Sinn Fein. Neither is a mere agitation or a theory turned into a party. Sinn Fein is the nation's expression of its identity and right to self-determination, and its mandate does not authorise it to declare for any specific programme save in so far as that programme proves to be the out-working of the self-determining nation. Once in history Capital stood for liberty. In the Polish war against Russia a hundred odd years ago, the capitalists – Jewish bankers – of Poland cast in their lot with the weaker side. Were the wonder to be repeated, and were Irish capitalists to stand in with the nation, Sinn Fein would accept their aid. But Irish patriotism has proved to be solely resident in the democracy, and Labour is the only party which has waived its private aims for the national cause. In the Labour movement, harmonising as it does with reviving Gaelicism, we see the nation determining itself. Sinn Fein, that asks all citizens to work for Ireland in their individual ways, is by its principles and nature bound to sanction the patriotic endeavours of the Labour Party, and to use the weapons which a truly national body places in its hands. By sheer force of patriotism, the Labour Party is engrossing political power, and by forming – let us not say the workers but, what is synonymous, the nation – into "One Big Union", it is forging the most powerful weapon ever held by the Gael. Before the united action of the One Big Union, English capitalism, and with it English political power,

* *Irish Times*, December 11th, 1918.

are to be rendered impotent. The one-day anti-conscription strike showed how a nation, wakened by Labour to a sense of its economic solidarity, even though deprived of political power, can assert its will.'*

And this is how the Labour Party puts it:

'The Russian Government was the only Government that had sincerely and whole-heartedly called for the self-determination of Ireland. Their British Government had not done it because it was capitalist. Their Yankee Government had not done it because it was capitalist. The German Government had not done it because it was capitalist too.'†

It would not be difficult to quote declarations by leaders of Sinn Fein which show how far it has moved towards the ideals of Revolutionary Labour. The Countess Markievics, who is a member of Dail Eireann and of the Supreme Grand Council, has openly declared for Soviet Government and the disfranchisement of all non-workers. Mr Figgis, who is one of the Secretaries of the Grand Council of Sinn Fein, depicts a somewhat similar constitutional evolution:

'Just as in the old State each council held authority in its own concerns, leaving to the monarch the co-ordination of the whole, so the modern councils would each rule their own affairs, subject to the control of the Assembly of the Nation. There would thus be two kinds of representations gathered together, the direct representation of the nation, *and there would be the special representation of the interests*, the union and pattern of which create the national life. Both would meet in the Government.'‡

Here we see, and not dimly, the Soviet idea, the Soldiers' and Sailors' Councils, and all the rest of the Bolshevist machinery, which, as has been recorded, were adumbrated by James Connolly a few years earlier.

It is, therefore, abundantly clear that whether by conviction or compulsion, Sinn Fein and Labour must be regarded as a single entity for the purpose of its revolutionary enterprise against Great Britain. Mr Robert Smillie showed his grasp of

* *Towards the Republic*, Chap. VI.

† Mr Cathal O'Shannon, Irish Labour Congress, November 1st, 1918.

‡ *The Gaelic State in the Past and Future*. The italics are ours.

realities when he called for a strong representation of Labour in Parliament on the ground that there would then be some inducement for Sinn Fein to go to 'that accursed reactionary chamber'. For then a bargain might be made on the basis of 'Your fight is our fight, come over and help us'.*

That Mr Smillie's words did not receive more attention when they were spoken must be ascribed partly to the delirium of the recent victory, partly to the preoccupation of the coming elections, and in larger degree to an inadequate appreciation of the realities of the Irish situation. For if they be considered coolly and with detachment they are full of significance. Let us review the facts of the position.

In Ireland there is a dual alliance between a party seeking political independence by revolutionary methods and a party seeking national independence, not only for its own sake, but as the prelude to the establishment of a Workers' Republic on the Russian model.

'To win for the workers of Ireland, collectively, the ownership and control of the whole produce of their labour.

'To secure the democratic management and control of all industries and services by the whole body of workers, manual and mental, engaged therein, in the interest of the nation and subject to the supreme authority of the national Government.'†

Between the revolutionary parties thus co-operating in Ireland and the Russian Soviet Republic there is an understanding as close and intimate as there was with Germany, an understanding thus described by the Countess Markievics:

'We have a treaty with Germany, the treaty Casement promoted. At the end of the war, if Germany is strong enough, she will make Ireland a free and independent Republic; and Casement gave an assurance that Ireland would be true to her deliverers.'‡

All these formalities have been observed in the arrangement between the Irish revolutionary parties and the Bolshevik Government. Dr McCartan has plighted the faith of Sinn Fein. The delegates of the Labour Party have waited upon and

* At Glasgow, December 6th, 1918.

† Objects and methods of the Irish Labour Party and Trade Union Congress. See 2*b* and *c*.

‡ Speech in East Tyrone, April 2nd, 1918.

exchanged fraternal greetings with Tchitcherin and Litvinoff, and have sealed the compact in the following passage of a statement on the international situation, unanimously adopted by the Irish Labour Party and Trades Union Congress:

'Finally, and true to its tradition for liberty, for internationalism, for the fraternity of the working-class of every land and for the Republic of the Workers, Irish Labour utters its vehement protest against the capitalist outlawry of the Soviet Republic of Russia, and calls upon the workers under the Governments sharing in this crime to compel the evacuation of the Republic, at the same time as it renews its welcome and congratulations to its Russian comrades *who for twelve months have exercised that political, social, and economic freedom towards which Irish workers in common with their fellows in other lands still strive and aspire.*'*

The Soviet Government on its side, through Mr Litvinoff, its ambassador to England, engaged to support Ireland's admission to the International as a nation. In making this promise Mr Litvinoff, who is said to have been well informed about Irish affairs, said that James Connolly's name was favourably known to the Russian Revolutionary Movement.†

These allies have an understanding, or compact – the exact word is immaterial – with the revolutionary section of British Labour, the party of direct action. Mr Smillie has proclaimed that he is willing to see Ireland established as an independent Republic in return for the assistance of Sinn Fein in the promotion of his theories. 'Your fight is our fight, come over and help us.' There is indeed an obstacle to this plan of campaign – the Sinn Fein vow of abstention from parliamentary action. But Mr Smillie, conscious that this vow might be retracted were revolutionary Labour represented in Parliament by two hundred and fifty men like himself or Mr John Maclean or Mr Robert Williams, holds out the active co-operation of Sinn Fein as an inducement to the electorate to support him and his friends.

Meanwhile, pending the electoral triumph for which he

* November 1st, 1918. From Report published by the authority of the executive. The italics are ours.

† Report by D. R. Campbell and William O'Brien, Trades Union Congress, August 5th, 1918.

hopes and works, the work of the allies is being carried on in the extra-Parliamentary field. The British extremists threaten the stoppage of British trade and industry in the interest of Bolshevist Russia, as witness the words of Mr John Maclean in the *Call* of January, 1919. Declaring that 'Bolshevism is Socialism triumphant', he proclaims it to be the duty of British revolutionary Socialists to hamper any attempts to impede its progress 'by developing the revolution in Britain not later than this year'.

The Soviet Republic despatches its emissaries to England, sets its printing presses to work striking off forged notes to dislocate British currency; and Russian roubles, not forged nor in the form of roubles, find their way to the revolutionary treasury.

And Sinn Fein 'does its bit' by keeping Ireland in a ferment, and watches events in Great Britain in order to seize its opportunity.

CHAPTER XIV

A STATE OF WAR

WITH the signing of the armistice a wave of social unrest and discontent swept over the country. Such a phenomenon is one of the sequelæ of all great wars, though perhaps seldom has it been so widespread and intense. Practically the whole industrial as well as the military strength of the nation had been mobilised, whence it came that there was no class of the workers left unaffected by uneasiness and uncertainty as to its future conditions. Add to this the prolonged tension of the war, the excessive strain of effort which it had demanded, and the disturbance of economic condition which it had caused, and it becomes easy to understand and condone a certain petulance and unreason among those whose work had come to a sudden end.

There were, however, elements in society which resolved to play upon this temper for their own ends. The pacifist cranks, the folk who boasted that 'they had no country' and during the war had proved it by siding with a foreign country against their own, people of a baser sort who had hired themselves to the enemy, agitators who lived by disorder – all saw a chance and proceeded to take it. German agents also saw their chance and proceeded to take it.

There were many things in the great war that astounded the minds of men and racked their nerves, but nothing was more astonishing or nerve-racking than the cobweb of intrigue, spun by a hidden hand, in which the nation was enmeshed, and in which it felt itself entangled at every crisis. Its most formidable and baffling manifestations occurred in connection with Labour. We have already seen how Baron Von Horst was subscribing liberally to support a great strike in the years before the war, and in similar manner during the war enemy agents were at work fomenting disaffection and promoting trouble in the factories and shipyards. The rank and file did not know it, they were unsuspecting tools. There were men higher up who knew it, and who talked of the rights of the workers while they were thinking of the interests of Germany. The process was not confined to Great Britain. In America Count Bernstorff was plotting sabotage with reliable agents; in Mexico the German Minister was stirring up trouble on the oilfields; while in Spain Prince Ratibor's efforts to promote strikes in the great mines evoked open denunciations in the Spanish Press. A careful study of the war will show a singular coincidence between industrial troubles in Allied or neutral countries and the contemporaneous interests of Germany.

So too when Germany fell. Her intrigues had failed to save her from falling, but they might yet serve to mitigate the effects of the fall. The engine was put in motion once more. A certain section in Great Britain made lofty appeals for generosity to the conquered in public, while in private they strove to foment a disorder which would enforce their open teaching. Further to create embarrassment, they proceeded to stir up revolt in order to preserve the existence of the Russian Soviet Government. It mattered nothing that that Government itself officially admitted that its executions were numbered by thousands, and that its own laws condemned millions to a slow death from inanition. 'Withdraw from Russia' became the battle-cry of the revolutionaries.

Professing a pure democracy, these extreme democrats proceeded to abjure their own faith. 'If the Coalition Government be returned,' roared Mr Smillie, 'I will use my influence to make the position of the Government untenable.' The London Workers' Committee, to whom the assurance was given, hailed it with rapture, and pointed out to Mr Smillie that he could best effect his purpose by bringing about a general stoppage of the mining industry as a protest against 'the violation of Russia'.*

Mr George Lansbury outlined a similar plan of campaign: 'If the Coalition wins . . . it will be the first duty of Labour . . . to put a term to the life of this Parliament. . . . The Constitution provides no remedy. Very well, then; we must seek one outside the Constitution. If we cannot persuade the Government, we

* Article in the *Workers' Dreadnought* by W. F. Watson, President of the London Workers' Committee. Quoted in the *Morning Post*, January 10th, 1919.

shall have to coerce it. And we have the means. . . . We must use our industrial power to regain our political liberty.'*

It is noteworthy that this threat was made before ever the new Parliament was elected, and that Mr Lansbury and his colleagues were prominent in their attempts to secure the most favourable terms for Germany.

The principal efforts of the revolutionaries were directed towards promoting revolt among the workers against their authorised leaders. Their policy and its results are thus described by Mr Jack Jones, a Labour Member whose principles are of a robust type:

'Some of the principal leaders of the unofficial strikes now taking place were well known anarchists, who were striving in every way to discredit organised political action, and if the workers of this country were prepared to follow their teaching, there would be reproduced here the trials and tribulations of the Russian and German peoples.'†

Such forebodings fell like sweet music on the ears of the Irish Republicans. Already they had begun to make ready to take the tide of social and industrial unrest at the flood. Early in November the Irish Labour Party had met; asserted the principle of national independence, and drawn up a constitution on the Soviet model. In the same month in which Mr Jones sounded his note of warning Mr Cathal O'Shannon and Mr Thomas Johnson were pleading the cause of Ireland at the International Labour and Socialist Conference at Berne, urging her claim to be admitted to the International as a national unit, expressing 'a fervent hope that the Bolshevik Revolution would uphold the purity of its noble principles against all its enemies', and declaring 'the people of Dublin to be at one with the people of Russia in accepting the programme of the Revolution'.‡

While Labour was thus consolidating the position of the Irish Republic abroad, Sinn Fein was preparing for its establishment by force at home. It may seem curious that Sinn Fein should be planning another rising at the same time that it was proclaiming its confidence that the Peace Conference would

* *The Herald*, Dec. 21st. 1918.

† *Morning Post*, February 7th, 1919.

‡ Official Report of Berne Conference. Published by the Irish Labour Party.

give Ireland her independence. But in fact that confidence was largely assumed. In their hearts De Valera and his colleagues must have nursed uneasy doubts whether they could make good the promises wherewith they had swept the constituencies. Boldly as they might cite the cases of Poland, Czecho-Slovakia, and Jugo-Slavia, old and decrepit organisms now emerging from Medea's cauldron in youthful vigour, on their own behalf, they must have known that the parallelism between them was defective. They must have known that they had not a friend at Paris: – not America, whose hospitality Ireland had abused; not Belgium, to whom Ireland had given a hospitality not distinguishable from hostility; not even Poland, nor Czecho-Slovakia, nor Serbia, on the side of whose mortal foes Ireland had ranged herself. Sinn Fein had obtained a pledge that Germany would represent its interests at the Conference, but when it became apparent that Germany was to have no voice in the deliberations the pledge became valueless, and Ireland was left without a champion.

In these dismal circumstances the labour troubles in Great Britain offered Sinn Fein an alternative road to success, and one moreover that, with good luck, might not be extraordinarily difficult. The Republicans placed their faith in the Triple Labour Alliance of Great Britain. The attitude of the railwaymen, miners, and transport workers was full of menace. If it should, as seemed not unlikely, develop into action, many of the obstacles to rebellion would be removed.

Such a strike, by stopping locomotion, would paralyse the military forces, and would localise military operations to the great advantage of the insurgents. It was, indeed, by no means certain that the unwitting aid of the 'Big Three' would not be more valuable to the Republicans than the assistance which Germany had been willing to give. To encourage the restless workers in Great Britain a strike was precipitated in Belfast by the Labour section of the Republican party, while Sinn Fein with feverish energy resumed its preparations for a military campaign.

Immediately after the General Election Sinn Fein proceeded to exploit the mandate of the constituencies. On January 4th Dr Patrick McCartan, under the style and title of Envoy of the Provisional Irish Government, notified all the Embassies and

Legations at Washington that Ireland had severed political relations with Great Britain on December 28th.* Thereafter the Republicans proclaimed that a state of war existed between Great Britain and Ireland, describing the military forces of the Crown as the Army of Occupation. Thus it is proclaimed in *An Toglac*, a newspaper printed and circulated secretly and widely through Ireland:

'It is the will of Ireland, expressed by her responsible Government, that a state of war shall be perpetuated in this country until the foreign garrison have evacuated our country. It will be the duty of the Volunteers, acting in accordance with the will of our Government and the wishes of the Irish people, to secure the continuance of that state of war by every means at our disposal, and in the most vigorous way practicable. Every Volunteer must be prepared for more drastic action, more strenuous activities, than ever before since Easter, 1916. As has several times been stated before, Volunteer officers must contemplate the possibilities of offensive as well as defensive action.'†

In the face of this declaration of war the bitter protests of the Republicans against the employment of the military forces in Ireland appear lacking both in logic and in that sense of humour with which the Irish race is generally credited. Whatever may be said against military intervention in civil troubles, there can be no question that soldiers are in their proper element in a state of war.

The history of Ireland can at all periods be pretty accurately followed through its criminal records. Analyse the activities of the White Boys, the Ribbonmen, the Land League, and the cattle-drivers, and it is possible to gauge with considerable exactitude the economic problems of their respective eras. And so with the history of the last year. The breaches of the law, and they were terribly numerous, proclaim the purpose of their authors with astonishing candour, and that purpose was civil war. Of the old agrarian outrage there is little; instead, we read of raids for arms and explosives, and of plans and methods for rebellion. Thus, Charles Hurley, who was tried by court-martial

* Wireless Press telegram from New York, January 4th: *Morning Post*, January 6th, 1919.

† Lord Chancellor's speech, House of Lords, April 14th, 1919.

at Cork on December 17th, 1918, had in his possession plans for the destruction of the police-barracks and post office at Castletown, Berehaven, as well as of the pier at that place where the British-American stores were housed. He also had plans for the destruction of roads and bridges leading to that important centre by gelignite and sulphine bombs. Michael Hoey, tried by court-martial at Galway on March 25th, was in possession of documents describing the best method of destroying railways and telegraphs, and of instructions for mining bridges and for attacking police-barracks.

There were numerous cases of attacks on police-barracks, houses, and individuals, all with the single object of capturing weapons and explosives. In the middle of February a body of men boarded a ship at Cork, and searched it for arms, by authority of 'a warrant from the Irish Republican Army'. An aerodrome at Collinstown, Co. Dublin, was attacked in the night about March 20th and eighty service rifles were carried off. Explosives were especially in demand, it being naturally the first object of the Republican tacticians to destroy all ways of communication. One of these enterprises deserves particular attention, both as being typical of the methods of Sinn Fein and because of its consequences.

By a happy coincidence, just as Sinn Fein was urgently searching for explosives, the Tipperary County Council requested the Government to provide it with a considerable quantity of gelignite for some blasting operations. The gelignite was sent from the store in Tipperary in the Council's carts, under convoy of two policemen, on January 20th. The Sinn Feiners were evidently apprised of the arrangements, for the convoy was attacked at Sologhead, a mile or two out of the town, by a party of men who promptly shot both constables dead and captured the gelignite, leaving the Council's employees unharmed to carry the news back to Tipperary. The district was declared a military area, an act which has been denounced as barbarous militarism by the very men who glorify the murder of the constables as an act of war. The Republicans replied with a counter-proclamation, which is given in full. Lest there should be any doubt, occasioned by its amazing character, of the official origin of this document, it may be compared with a speech made by Mr Roger Sweetman, M.P. for North Wexford, at Gorey on January 5th:

'Any one who did England's dirty work, let him be lord-lieutenant, judge, or policeman, he would tell them that they would treat them as enemies of the country thenceforward.'*

It may also be noted that thirty copies of this Proclamation were found in the possession of Michael Duggan, a Sinn Feiner, belonging to County Tipperary.

'PROCLAMATION.

'Whereas a foreign and tyrannical Government is preventing Irishmen exercising the civil right of buying and selling in their own markets in their own country, and

'Whereas almost every Irishman who has suffered the death penalty for Ireland was sentenced to death solely on the strength of the evidence and reports of policemen, who therefore are dangerous spies, and

'Whereas the thousands of Irishmen who have been deported and sentenced solely on the evidence of these same hirelings and assassins and traitorous spies, the police, and

'Whereas the life, limb and living of no citizen of Ireland is safe while these paid spies are allowed to infest the country, and

'Whereas it has come to our knowledge that some men and boys have been arrested and drugged, and

'Whereas there are few Irishmen, who have sunk to such depths of degradation, that they are prepared to give information about their neighbours and fellow countrymen to the police, and

'Whereas all these evils will continue just so long as the people permit:

'We hereby proclaim the South Riding of Tipperary a military area with the following regulations:

'(*a*) A policeman found within the said area on and after the – day of February, 1919, will be deemed to have forfeited his life. The more notorious police being dealt with as far as possible first.

'(*b*) On and after the – day of February, 1919, every person in the pay of England (magistrates, jurors, etc.) who helps

* *Freeman's Journal*, January 7th, 1919.

England to rule this country or who assists in any way the upholders of the foreign Government of this South Riding of Tipperary, will be deemed to have forfeited his life.

'(*c*) Civilians who give information to the police or soldiery, especially such information as is of a serious character, if convicted will be executed, *i.e.* shot or hanged.

'(*d*) Police, doctors, prison officials who assist at or who countenance, or who are responsible for, or who are in any way connected with the drugging of an Irish citizen for the purpose of obtaining information, will be deemed to have forfeited his life, and may be hanged or drowned, or shot at sight as a common outlaw. Offending parties will be executed should it take years to track them down.

'(*e*) Every citizen must assist when required in enabling us to perform our duty.

'By Order.'

This Proclamation merits particular attention as embodying the methods by which the Republic of Ireland enforces its authority, the same methods of *Schrecklichkeit* on which German militarism relied for the administration of Belgium. It is not a dead letter, a mere *brutum fulmen,* a thing of sound and fury signifying nothing. Its warnings have been fulfilled. A County Inspector of Constabulary has been murdered while altering the hands of his clock to summer time; the Estate Commissioners in Clare have been threatened with death if they allot land to ex-soldiers; a respectable man in County Galway has had his house fired into because his children attended a school which was under the Republican ban!* The Countess Markievics has preached the boycotting of policemen's children; constables and soldiers are waylaid and attacked. In the South Riding of Tipperary itself, since the proclamation has been issued, two constables were murdered in a train as Knocklong Station in the presence of the passengers and railway officials, and the prisoner in their custody was rescued. District-Inspector Hunt was shot dead in the crowded market place of Thurles, and his murderers walked quietly away unmolested.

* These cases were mentioned by the Chief Secretary for Ireland in the House of Commons.

The agents of Sinn Fein always are unmolested. The people dare not speak nor jurors convict. The long arm of Sinn Fein reaches everywhere and its hand is laid upon the nation's lips. There is no great mystery about these deeds, their perpetrators are very frequently well known, but sympathy or fear keeps men silent.

While Sinn Fein was thus preparing for armed rebellion in anticipation of a great labour upheaval in Great Britain, the left wing of the Republican party was busily engaged cementing the Bolshevik alliance at Berne, promoting British industrial unrest through its agents in England and Scotland, and promoting serious labour troubles in Belfast, both as an embarrassment to the Irish Government and as an encouragement to the revolutionaries on the other side of the Channel. Mr Thomas Johnson has set forth the hopes and policy of the Republicans with commendable frankness. Explaining why the Limerick strike failed and was bound to fail, he yet approved it because 'there were always the possibilities or probabilities that aggressive action in Ireland might prompt aggressive action on the other side'.*

Mr Bernard Doyle has thus expounded the joint plan of campaign in Dublin:

'The voice of the Irish people, as expressed at the polls, had given them authority to demand the release of the men and women unjustly held in English jails. The workers of Ireland were behind them and, speaking as a trade unionist, he was glad to say that they were prepared to "down tools" at any minute in this matter at the command of the Irish Republic.'†

The opportunity presented itself some three months later. There was in Limerick prison a man named Byrne, who was serving a term of hard labour. He went on hunger strike, and was removed on March 12th to the hospital of the workhouse, which is on the Clare side of the river Shannon. Here he remained for some weeks in charge of a prison warder and an armed body of Constabulary. Saturday is the visiting day at the hospital and visitors are admitted freely between 1.30 and 3.30 p.m. On Saturday, April 6th, a party of twenty to thirty men

* Speech at Irish Trade Congress. *Cork Examiner*, August 6th, 1919.

† *Irish Independent*, January 6th, 1919.

rushed into the ward where Byrne was confined, guarded by the warder and five policemen. A fierce revolver duel followed. One policeman was killed, another dangerously wounded, as were all the other constables and the warder, though less seriously. The rescue party then departed, taking with them Byrne, who had himself been wounded in the fight, and whose dead body was found a few days later in a cottage a couple of miles distant.

The Government met this 'act of war' by proclaiming Limerick a military area. Under these regulations permits were required to enter or leave the city, and it therefore became necessary for workers who lived across the river to obtain passes in order to go to their work. Such permits were readily obtainable, and many employers obtained them for their men. But this did not suit the workers, who saw a chance of striking a blow in support of Sinn Fein. A general strike was proclaimed. The Roman Catholic Bishop and clergy published a statement that 'the proclaiming of Limerick under existing circumstances was quite unwarrantable'.

The National Labour Executive took the matter up. Mr Cathal O'Shannon* urged on the Irish Socialist Party the advisability of establishing Soviet Government in Ireland. Mr Johnson, his colleague at Berne, hastened to Limerick to try the experiment there, while Mr O'Shannon went to England to enlist the aid of the Socialist extremists, whom he met at Sheffield.

He told his sympathetic audience, the Conference of the British Socialist Party, the moving tale of how the 'Limerick Soviet' had struck against 'a military occupation'. He called for 'a combination of all the elements of the Left in South Wales, Ireland, England, and Scotland to bring about by their united efforts an alliance of revolutionary Socialists, and thus end the white terror now prevailing'. The Conference sent a message of greeting to their fellow-workers in Limerick 'struggling for civil liberty against the military authorities in Ireland'.

That they did nothing more must have been disappointing to the Limerick Soviet, which was already printing notes, varying from one to ten shillings, in anticipation of the Great Day,

* *Freeman's Journal*, April 14th, 1919.

an act which was approved with great enthusiasm by the Congress of the Independent Labour Party at Huddersfield.

Mr Thomas Johnson has revealed how great a disappointment it was to the Republican leaders. A national strike, he says, would have resulted in armed revolt. The National Executive actually proposed that Limerick should be evacuated by all its inhabitants, 'leaving an empty shell in the hands of the military'.* The local Soviet, however, rejected the proposal, and the Limerick strike fizzled out, because, as Mr Johnson put it in the speech just quoted, 'there was no probability of a responsive movement in England and Scotland',

*

Here ends our survey of the Irish revolutionary movement. But the movement itself has not reached its appointed end. In Ireland its desultory warfare still goes on; in Great Britain it still works to obtain that 'responsive movement' which Mr Johnson holds is essential to its success.

The overt action of Sinn Fein in London is carried on under the ægis of the Self-Determination League, but its real activities are on a lower and darker plane. Time was when it found its allies in the Fellowship of Reconciliation. The Sinn Fein badge and colours, white, green, and yellow, were to be seen at the Friends' Meeting-house in Bishopsgate, where the Fellows of Reconciliation denounced self-defence because 'human life is a sacred thing and war abhorrent in the sight of God', while they would go to Ireland, inspect Madame Markievics' Sinn Fein scouts – the British Boy Scout movement was condemned as 'tending to foster militarism' – and extol 'the armed guards of honour which they saw parading to do honour to the leaders of Easter, 1916'.

Among the members of the Fellowship were a large number of Irishmen holding appointments in a certain public office. In England they held classes to create conscientious objectors, and mock trials to instruct them in the art of defence should they be made to suffer for conscience sake. In Ireland they adopted

* Speech at Irish Labour and Trade Union Party Congress. *Daily News*, August 6th, 1919.

sterner methods. Large numbers applied for leave in the spring of 1916. Some never came back; it is alleged that many of those who did return bore traces, and still bear them, of having left their conscientious objections to militancy behind them at Holyhead.

At present the principal societies in London with which Sinn Fein works are the London Workers' Committee, of which Mr W. F. Watson is the head, and the Workers' Socialist Federation, over which Miss Sylvia Pankhurst presides.

This latter organisation is very cosmopolitan in character. Miss Pankhurst is a very ardent and outspoken champion of Bolshevism, and all who aim at the overthrow of society find a meeting-place in Old Ford Road. There shall we find the female Sinn Fein orator, whose oratorical excesses have earned for her a martyr's crown of eleven days' imprisonment; the lady who calls herself Belgian, but who has nephews in the Bolshevik army, who contributes to the *Dreadnought*, the organ of the Federation, paragraphs from the most advanced Communist journals of Europe, such as *Avanti* and *La Vague*, and who occupies her scanty leisure in working for the Russian Information Bureau; and on occasion Mrs Sheehy Skeffington. There too might be found one James McGrath, a railway clerk in the Camden Town Goods office, until his activities were cut short in February last, when he was sentenced to six months' imprisonment for attempting to send pistols to Ireland.

Thither also come at intervals mysterious Russians, bringing advice and comfort and what is euphemistically described as 'assistance'. One such attended the meeting of the Federation last Whitsuntide, grateful for the skill with which he had been smuggled in, and concealed, and imparting much interesting information about the Third International and the methods of Russian Bolshevism in return. In reply Miss Pankhurst spoke of the honour done the Federation in having a delegate sent to its Annual Congress direct from the Soviet Government of Russia.

The Workers' Socialist Federation, indeed, has always owed much to distinguished foreigners. In its early days it secured the patronage and pecuniary assistance of an old friend, Baron Von Horst. When he was detected in the distribution of seditious literature in Ireland and interned, his friend Miss Lillian

Troy, following the direction of his sympathies, gave Miss Pankhurst the use of the Orpheum Cinema Theatre at Croydon. This place at once became a centre of revolutionary propaganda. Mrs Sheehy Skeffington spoke, under the Sinn Fein flag, to an audience largely composed of Russian Jews. In the same hall David Ramsay made a speech for which he got six months' imprisonment.

The London Workers' Committee is the London counterpart of the Clyde Workers' Committee. Its programme is the destruction of parliamentary government, and therefore it is not surprising that the Sinn Feinn badge is largely in evidence at its meetings. This organisation claims the authorship of many strikes during the war, notably the engineering strike in May 1917, which stopped work at Erith, Woolwich, and other munition centres at a highly critical period. At the Holborn Empire on December 1st, 1918, Mr Watson boasted that he had formed the nucleus of two hundred Soviets, that he had corrupted many Irish soldiers, and that the London Sinn Feiners could supply him with several hundred men trained in the use of arms.

This gentleman's revolutionary career suffered a temporary check in consequence of an indiscreet speech at the Albert Hall on February 8th. On that occasion the platform was decorated with the Sinn Fein tricolour and the Red Flag, and among the speakers were John Maclean, the Bolshevik Consul at Glasgow, Mr Israel Zangwill, who has since endeavoured with very indifferent success to explain away his presence and his speech, and Mrs Sheehy Skeffington, who said that the two nations who had done best in the war were Russia and Ireland – Russia because she had ceased to fight and Ireland because she had resisted conscription.

The offices of the London Workers' Committee are shared by the Soldiers', Sailors' and Airmen's Union, a frankly seditious organisation, run by a man who got up a meeting at Folkestone last January, when the Colours of the Guards had to be brought back to London, and who, in consequence of the exploit, gained the favour of the *Daily Herald*. Later the Union started a movement to induce the Derby recruits to desert on the ground that their term of service had expired, and was in consequence turned out of its offices in Whitefriars Street as an undesirable tenant. This organisation, like Mr Lansbury, had a great deal to do with the attempted police strike of the present summer, and is a favourite rallying point for Bolsheviks, discontented soldiers, conscientious objectors, and Sinn Feiners.

CHAPTER XV

CONCLUSIONS

PREVIOUS writers have called attention to the persistence and continuity of the Irish revolutionary movement. It has been the purpose of this book to show that the Irish Republicanism of today, though in lineal descent from the insurgents of the past, aiming at the same goal, and sharing with them certain attributes common to all insurrectionary organisations, yet differs from them in many particulars of the highest and most urgent importance in their bearing upon the Irish problem and its solution.

The present movement represents, indeed, in great measure a revolt against its predecessors. It is inspired by the conviction of their futility, which it holds was due to the fact that the old revolutionists, though they knew what they wanted, did not really know why they wanted it or how it could be gained. They had an aim, but it was not a conscious aim, and therefore all their efforts became of no effect. They hated British rule, but because they never clearly grasped the reason for hating it, their hatred never carried them far. And, what in the eyes of the modern Republicans is worse, a purpose based on hatred tends to become blurred and dim as memory grows dull.

To meet this grave defect the Gaelic League and Sinn Fein sought to revive a positive principle – nationality – through the medium of the Irish language. For the language itself, outside a few enthusiasts or sentimentalists, they may have had but small regard; their devotion to it has been mainly due to the belief – possibly well founded – that the National Idea which it would generate would do more to keep alive the spirit of revolt than the negative principle of hatred which had inspired the insurrectionary movements of the past.

While men like Dr Hyde and Professor MacNeill thus sought to inspire the National Movement with an intellectual soul, the more practical Mr Arthur Griffith set himself to develop a spirit of national commercialism, not only as an object good in itself, but as a most effective weapon against British domination. Irish Nationalism was to have its own banks, its own Law Courts* and schools, its own consular service, mainly because thus would be asserted the principle of a separate nationality.

In like manner did James Connolly strive to advance the interests of the proletariat. Industrial freedom, he taught, was indissolubly linked up with national independence. In a free Ireland only could the Irish workers be free; freedom for the workers of Ireland would be incomplete unless their country also were relieved of its shackles.

The introduction of this positive assertion of nationality marks a great advance, and differentiates the new movement from the old in a surprising degree. In the first place it promotes persistency of effort. Nothing is more noticeable in the old rebellions than their spasmodic manifestations. The rising of 1798, 1848, and 1867 were short-lived. With their defeat the movement died away, not to reappear for a cycle of years. During the intervening periods men who had been conspirators became constitutional reformers, some abandoned revolution altogether, others became valued servants of the Crown against which they had conspired. The spirit which moved them to violence appeared to be rather the effervescence of hot-blooded youth than a solemn and deliberate policy.

Movements so inspired could be crushed without difficulty when they broke ground; there was always the hope on one side and the fear on the other that by the reform of abuses, by reparation for old wrongs, by generous legislation, the underlying hostility might be weakened. And, as a fact, these hopes and fears were to a great extent justified by events. Compared with the rebellion of 1798, the risings of Smith O'Brien and James Stephens were little more than riots. The revolutionary fever seemed to be burning itself out; the idea of national independence appeared to be moving towards the academic stage and to be becoming a tradition rather than a principle.

The new Nationalism has changed all that. It takes no account

* The *Cork Examiner* of September 16th contains a report of a Sinn Fein Arbitration Court which adjudicated on a question of the sale of an estate.

of the history of British rule, it takes account only of the fact of British rule. It is as little revengeful for past wrongs – and there have been wrongs – as it is grateful for benefits – and they are neither small nor few.

'Our Nationalism is not founded upon grievances. We are opposed not to English misgovernment, but to English government in Ireland.'*

Here, then, we are face to face with an abiding principle of insurgency. Evil memories may be transient, withered by time or effaced by gratitude, but hatred of a fact persists so long as the fact continues.

To perceive the operation of this spirit it needs only to read Irish history since Easter 1916. Such a defeat as was inflicted on the rebels in that year would have crushed previous revolutionary movements for half a century. It did not check the new Nationalism for a month. With their leaders dead or in prison, the Republicans were planning a new rebellion for the following year. When that effort failed, they set themselves to foil every attempt at conciliation, and succeeded.

In former times the irreconcilable conspirators, when their plans went awry, withdrew into obscurity to prepare new conspiracies. The new Nationalists, on the contrary, have come out more boldly into the light of day, establishing a National Parliament and issuing the prospectus of a National Loan, the interest of which shall become payable on the international recognition of the Irish Republic.

They have proclaimed a state of war, and are carrying on a guerilla warfare of a peculiarly barbarous character. There have been periods of barbarous crime in Ireland's troubled history. But in the worst of those periods there was some ostensible motive for the barbarity. A landlord might be suspected of severity, a farmer might be held in abhorrence for taking an evicted farm, a man might be regarded as an informer or traitor, there might be some personal or family feud – there were many motives which could never excuse the crime, but which might, at least, explain it.

There is no such explanation, no such excuse as 'the wild

* See p. 194.

justice of revenge,' for the crimes of today. They are not wanton, they are cold and calculated; they are not the outcome of personal passion, they are 'the diabolical work of an organisation.'* Recalling the terms of the Proclamation issued by Sinn Fein and quoted in a previous chapter, the organisation which directs such deeds can readily be indentified. And so in Ireland today no man is safe, whatever be his character or innocency of life, if he stands in the way of the new Nationalism by reason of his attachment to British rule, or by his willingness to discharge the ordinary duties of a citizen.

There is no weakness or wavering in the ranks of the Irish Republicans. They speak, not as defeated rebels, but as men dictating terms to a conquered enemy. They do not even deign to parley with Great Britain, or to offer her Ireland's friendship in return for Ireland's freedom. Such language was held by the revolutionists of the past: those of the present are more inexorable. To them Great Britain is not only a country from whose rule they desire to escape, but a country which must be brought down in headlong ruin. In India, in Egypt, in South Africa, wherever England has a vulnerable spot or disaffected subjects, these are the places and the people for which Sinn Fein has the most special regard and to which it is most profuse in its promises of help.

It is not, however, on its intellectual and political side that the new movement is most sharply differentiated from the old. Infinitely more novel and more menacing are its economic developments, not only by reason of their intrinsic nature, but in their effect upon any possible proposals for a settlement of the Irish question. Those proposals range from the grant of complete independence, favoured by Mr Childers, to some such form of self-government as is contained in the Home Rule Act. To discuss the merits of any of them is outside the purview of this volume, but it would have been written in vain were the facts which it describes not taken into account in the consideration of them.

The precise relation between Sin Fein and Labour are not easy to calculate, but there are certain phenomena which

* Rev. Thomas MacBrien, C.C. Letter written in reference to the murder of Sergeant Brady, and published in the *Dublin Daily Express*, September 17th, 1919. Mr MacBrien is a Roman Catholic priest.

suggest that they are intimate, more intimate perhaps than is suspected by those who talk glibly of settling the Irish question by constitutional concession.

Although Sinn Fein means self-reliance, it is the settled policy of the Sinn Feiners to attain their main object through foreign aid. Germany has failed them; America is alternately threatened and cajoled, but in their inmost hearts the Irish Republicans are doubtful of success in that direction. Failing America, there remains not a single nation that can help; but there does remain a revolutionary system, an Ishmael of humanity, whose only hope of existence lies in the fomentation of revolt against established order. The Russian Soviet Republic, seeking to break down surrounding capitalistic institutions, and even Socialist institutions if they connote stability or conformity to established doctrines of government, is itself seeking for allies in every direction, and so to Moscow Ireland turns her eyes and addresses her appeals.

Naturally the Irish Labour Party is the chief instrument of such negotiations. But Sinn Fein itself, whatever be its secret views of Bolshevik doctrine, has also yielded to the pressure of necessity. The conversations and correspondence of Dr MacCartan and Mr Liam Mellowes with Mr L. Martens* cannot be disregarded in this connection.

That there is an understanding between the Irish Republicans and the Bolshevik revolutionists is beyond question. We have seen how their emissaries are always in close touch with the British extremists.† And it has been shown how periods of Labour unrest in Great Britain have synchronised with outbursts of crime and outrage in Ireland. The coincidences are too marked to be accidental. Nor is it possible to resist the conclusion that the Irish Republicans are in receipt of monetary assistance from Russia. The operations of Sinn Fein are costly. Seven years ago it was penniless; today it wields a huge organisation, runs newspapers, purchases arms and munitions of war, keeps its representatives abroad, and maintains an army of officials at home. Even its hired assassins are supplied with motor-cars. It gets money somewhere, and the Soviet Republic

* See Chap. XIII.
† See Chap. XIV.

is known to be spending large sums in foreign propaganda. The fact is not concealed. Bela Kun is not the only alien revolutionary who has received grants from the Soviet Treasury. It is known that money has reached this country, but Miss Pankhurst only accounts for a small part of it. And it is not to be overlooked that, in the revelations lately made by the police authorities, the name of Mr L. Martens occurs as one of those who are prominently concerned in this Bolshevik propaganda – Mr Martens, with whom MacCartan and Mellowes are in intimate relations.

The inference will, of course, be stoutly denied. But so were the financial transactions between Sinn Fein and Bernstorff denied in Dublin – and admitted in Berlin.

It is possible, it is even probable, that among the members of Sinn Fein there are many who view these economic tendencies with aversion and apprehension. But, much as they fear the movement, they are powerless to stop it, as throughout history the moderates have always been captured by the extremists. Revolutions, it has been said, devour their children; Mirabeau always gives way to Marat.

It results from this that schemes of settlement, designed to placate the moderates of Sinn Fein, are foredoomed to failure for the reason that the moderates no longer count. One may go even further, and say that schemes of settlement which might attract the more stalwart adherents of Sinn Fein have very little chance of success. There was, as we have seen, a time when Mr Griffith might have accepted the Constitution of 1782 in satisfaction of his demands,* though it might not have satisfied the majority of his colleagues. That time, as Mr O'Hegarty says, has gone; but even had it not gone, such a proposal would be rejected by the Labour wing of the Republican Party, and by those – not a few – of the Sinn Feiners who stand with them.

In formulating his economic policy and constructing his party of revolutionary Labour, Connolly appealed to sentiment and self-interest. In the former – the reference to the old Celtic communal system – he sought the inspiration of his movement, in the latter its driving force. That force lies in the belief, which

* See Chap. III.

he so strenuously inculcated, that all the old Irish patriotic movements had broken down because they took no account of the interests of the workers. Especially had the constitutional patriots betrayed the interests of the proletariat, keeping alive and exploiting their wrongs for their own selfish political purpose. While the revolutionary movements had not been guilty of such black treachery, and had even in some cases caught glimpses of the truth, they too had failed because their direction had fallen into the hands of the capitalists and the *bourgeoisie.* If Labour, then, is to reap any reward for its Nationalism and any security for itself, it must look, in the words of Wolfe Tone, 'to that respectable class – the men of no property.'

The proletarian wing of the Republican Movement is, therefore, unalterably pledged to oppose any settlement on constitutional lines. Even were it not so pledged, its adhesion to Bolshevism would make the acceptance of constitutional conditions impossible. Already there are signs that Labour is somewhat distrustful of the more moderate Republicans and is determined to impose its will upon the movement.

The growth and influence of Irish Bolshevism must be taken into serious account in any review of the Irish problem and in any remedial measures for its solution. A Bolshevist Ireland would be a constant menace to the social and industrial peace of Great Britain. For all modern creeds Bolshevism is necessarily the most aggressive. There is no place in a community of States based on social order for a State founded upon anarchy. Static conditions are fatal to its existence; it must proselytise or perish.

Such is the position of Ireland today, and all because five years ago, when the path of constitutional self-government within the British Empire lay broad and smooth before her, she took the wrong turning. The road she then chose has led her into wastes whereof no man can see the end. To all who would help to guide her back to the point from which she went astray she turns blind eyes and deaf ears. To all who approach her with offers of conciliation she replies with Jehu, 'What hast thou to do with peace? Turn thee behind me.' On one point only is there agreement between the warring factions – that there can be no agreement. 'There is no half-way house between Union and Separation,' says Sir Edward Carson at Belfast. And across the Atlantic, like an echo, comes De Valera's response. 'There is no half-way house between Union and Separation.'

THE GREEN BERET

by
Hilary St. George Saunders

For their raids and battles far behind the enemy lines in the Mediterranean, North Africa and Burma, the men in the Green Beret have become a legend.

This book tells the truth behind that legend.

NEW ENGLISH LIBRARY

THE MAN

by Irving Wallace

'I, Douglass Dilman, do solemnly swear that I will faithfully execute the office of President of the United States, and will, to the best of my ability, preserve, protect, and defend the constitution of the United States.'

It is unthinkable, unimaginable – the fourth President after John F. Kennedy is a full-blooded Negro. This fearful honour falls on him not by the will of the people, but through accidental death and a law of succession never before invoked. Dilman must prove to be a man with a worth of his own . . .

The tremendous drama of a man on trial for his race sweeps through the lives of those connected with him: the suave, ambitious Secretary of State, next in line to the Presidency; Dilman's beautiful social secretary, who accuses him of attempted rape; his son, secretly a member of a subversive organisation; his daughter, passing for white; and the woman the widowed President loves yet dare not marry.

NEW ENGLISH LIBRARY